What People Are Saying About
The Power and Purpose of Singleness...

"The hand of God is on Mike Cavanaugh to help the Church reach and touch what many believe to be the most dynamic group sharing today's culture—singles population."

—*Dr. Jack Hayford, President*
International Church of the Foursquare Gospel

"No message or person I know has had a deeper and more long-lasting impact on single adults than this book and Mike Cavanaugh. From his life, integrity, and long experience in helping people, Mike has a refreshing and unique way of inspiring people to a life of fulfillment, purpose, and selfless service."

—*Dean Sherman, International Dean*
College of Christian Ministries, University of the Nations

"Mike Cavanaugh has spoken at Fishnet festivals on a number of occasions and has always brought an inspiring word from God. He is a passionate speaker, an excellent communicator, and a joy to work with. His passion for the spiritual needs of singles is keenly sensed when he speaks."

—*Larry D. Andes, President,*
Fishnet Ministries, Inc.

"This is a remarkable book that will help set you free to serve God. Michael has been used of the Lord to mobilize thousands of single adults to change the world for Jesus. I have seen the fruit of his ministry firsthand at our festivals, his church, and even in China. His wisdom and biblical insights are going to encourage and bless you."

—*Rev. Dr. Harry L. Thomas, Jr., Cofounder,*
Director of Creation Festivals

"When I heard Mike speak about undivided devotion, my whole attitude was transformed. His message spoke to the core of my need and answered the critical questions about my heart that I had been unable to ask. I needed to rededicate myself completely to Jesus."

—Nancy "Honeytree" Miller, recording artist,
composed the song "Single Heart"
after hearing Cavanaugh speak

"It is not easy to be single in a secular culture that affirms lifestyles and choices that are wholly inconsistent with traditional Christian values. This book is a great read and a valuable guide for any single who would navigate those dangerous waters to live his or her life in the fullness of the blessing of Christ. Our European Betel communities and churches have enjoyed and been edified by Mike's wisdom and wit. We have found him to be one of the most effective contemporary communicators who speaks to youths and single adults today. Anyone who would understand the single's heart should read *The Power and Purpose of Singleness*."

—Elliott Tepper, Senior Pastor,
Iglesia Betel of Madrid,
President of Betel International,
Field Leader of WEC-Betel Transnational

"I know of no one who speaks or writes with more authority and impact to the young generation than Michael Cavanaugh. His ministry has had a profound impact on my own life."

—Derek Joseph Levendusky, Lead singer,
Isaiah Six

The Power and Purpose of Singleness

The Power and Purpose of Singleness

FINDING FULFILLMENT AS A SINGLE ADULT

WHITAKER
HOUSE

THE POWER AND PURPOSE OF SINGLENESS:
Finding Fulfillment as a Single Adult

ISBN: 978-1-60374-099-9
Printed in the United States of America
© 2009 by Michael Cavanaugh

Whitaker House
1030 Hunt Valley Circle
New Kensington, PA 15068
www.whitakerhouse.com

No publication of this material would be complete without recognizing the contribution of Susan McCarthy Palmer for editing and compiling much of this text, especially the study guide. I will always be grateful for her help in making this book possible.

Library of Congress Cataloging-in-Publication Data

Cavanaugh, Michael, 1954–
    The power and purpose of singleness : finding fulfillment as a single adult / by Michael Cavanaugh.
        p. cm.
    Summary: "An interactive explanation of how God can use singleness to bring a person closer to Him and uniquely equip that person for service"—Provided by publisher.
    ISBN 978-1-60374-099-9 (trade pbk. : alk. paper) 1. Single people—Religious life. I. Title.
    BV4596.S5C38 2008
    248.8'4—dc22
                            2008037348

1 2 3 4 5 6 7 8 9 10 11 ᴜᴊ 16 15 14 13 12 11 10 09

FOREWORD

I was twenty-seven and single when I suddenly became aware that God might be calling me to a life of singleness for Him.

I wondered, *What would that mean to me? What would I be missing? What would others think? Would I be looked on as a reject, or as an opportunity for the church would-be matchmaker? What about temptation? My sexuality? What purpose could my singleness possibly fulfill? Does God really call some to a life of singleness, or is it due to a flaw? Am I a leftover or "second best"?*

These and many other questions demanded an answer! And as I wrestled with these quandaries and struggled to come to a place of resolve in those younger days, I longed for someone to speak to the subject.

Today, someone has—Mike Cavanaugh! In this book, Mike cuts to the heart of the issue and presents scriptural answers—real-life answers that come from a wealth of experience in counseling, ministering with, and leading singles.

While reading this manuscript, I began to walk through my own history as a single starting a missionary organization. As I came to rest in God's will, He led me to meet and marry Darlene, a nurse who, by choice, had a career and fulfillment as a single.

As I read, I also pondered some of those I have met who have influenced my life and were called to singleness: Corrie ten Boom, Bill Gothard, Basilea Schlink, Mother Teresa, and others. How did

I perceive them? Not as less than normal! And certainly not as leftovers. They were people of destiny!

You, too, are a person of incredible potential and destiny. Although this book relates to your singleness, you will discover singleness is neither the problem nor even the true issue! Destiny— God's and yours—fulfillment—God's and yours—is the issue. That's what this book and your life are all about.

—Loren Cunningham
Founder, Youth With a Mission International

TABLE OF CONTENTS

INTRODUCTION:
A SPRINGBOARD INTO SERVICE

SINCE THE ORIGINAL PUBLICATION OF THIS BOOK, THOUsands upon thousands of singles have been transformed by its message and hundreds of churches have used it as a textbook for Sunday school classes and singles discussion groups.

This new edition of the book is more conducive than ever to personal and small-group studies. Each chapter ends with a "Transitional Thought" before the Study Guide that personally illustrates or further enhances the subject matter dealt with in that chapter. It is hoped that these stories will increase the reader's understanding of the issues dealt with in a particular chapter and even provoke further discussion of those issues.

The "Study Guide" section at the end of each chapter is a tool to help individuals and groups retain the principles of this life-changing primer on living as Christian singles in today's world, add to their understanding of God's purpose for them as single adults, and help them apply the truths that will set them free to serve God with their whole hearts.

Filled with questions that prompt examination of the singles scene today and an individual's heart toward God, as well as activities that invite you to delve deeper into God's Word and step practically into service, this study guide is a tool that activates the mighty to perform exploits for God in their generation. Read it. Use it. And be used by God today!

How to Use the Study Guide

The study guide was designed to reinforce teachings covered in the book, as well as to help the reader apply them to his or her own life. There are two main categories in each study guide:

1. **Questions for Knowing and Growing**. This section is designed to reinforce the teachings found in the book. When questions require a specific answer included in the book, write out the answer as expressed in the book. If the answer is too long, you may write the answer in an abridged form, using your own words. Page numbers are provided to the left of the questions to help you locate the relevant material from the preceding chapter.

Questions marked with a small arrow (▶) are "think" questions, designed to "pull out" your own thoughts on an issue discussed in the book. Our purpose in offering these questions is to help you relate what you've read in the book to your own life and apply it. Discussion group leaders may wish to center their programs around these questions for lively participation by all.

2. **Doing the Word**. This section suggests some ideas that, by application, will reinforce, augment, and put into practice the teachings contained in the book. Some are for individual use; others are more applicable with groups. The hope is that the individual will choose to become involved in both types of projects; the activities involving groups will not only help them grow individually but also in their roles as a members of the corporate body of Christ.

Before You Begin

Before you begin this book, we ask that you take a moment to write out what you believe to be God's will for you as a single person. We will ask you to do this again at the end of the book in the hope that the comparison between the two will help to reinforce what you've learned about the power and purpose of singleness and help you to start walking in that calling today.

God's will for me as a single adult:

_____

_____

_____

_____

_____

_____

_____

_____

_____

_____

_____

_____

_____

_____

_____

_____

_____

_____

_____

_____

_____

_____

_____

_____

_____

_____

_____

_____

_____

_____

_____

_____

You Are Not Half a Cookie

H AVE YOU EVER HAD THE FEELING THAT YOU WERE less than a person? Somehow, as Jane married Joe, Denise married Mark, and Pam married Jim, you began to feel like a left-over in life or the last person picked for a baseball team.

You remember how it was in school. Two kids stood in front of a group of their peers and, one by one, picked people for their team. Slowly the crowd began to get smaller and smaller, until "the crowd" became a group, and "the group" became a few.

You watched nervously as the group dwindled. Inside, you shouted, "Pick me! Oh, pick me! Oh, *please* pick me." You didn't want to be the last person picked—the one the other guy took because he had to.

Finally, the dreaded moment came. There you stood with another unathletic-looking person. Neither of you was a prime pick. But if you could be the last person *chosen*—there was a fifty-fifty chance now, the best odds yet—then at least you would retain a little self-respect.

The last choice was made. It wasn't you. The other person heaved a big sigh of relief while you lowered your shoulders, bowed your head, and slunk over to the team that *had to take you.* You didn't even want to look at them. You could just imagine how everyone was taking this. It was like getting Charlie Brown. You were the death blow to the team—a leftover.

Many singles feel that way about their singleness. They feel rejected, hurt, and inferior. *There's got to be something wrong with me,* they think. *Look at Jane. Look at Terri. Look at Tom. They all have somebody. What's wrong with me? I'm still single.*

Sometimes, family and friends reinforce these negative feelings. They try to pair singles off or infer they're somehow less than other adults simply because they aren't married. "When are you going to settle down?" parents moan, as though the only balanced, rooted lifestyle could be found in marriage.

Many churches and para-church ministries take a similar position. They embrace the widely held opinion that ultimate fulfillment comes through marriage and end up selling singles short in the process.

When I began thinking about ministering to single adults, I did a lot of research on what was done for them already. What I found disturbed me. Many churches and ministries missed the mark in coping with what they called the "single adult problem."

Almost consistently, they saw themselves either as social directors or psychiatrists. They concentrated all their efforts on providing recreational activities for the "unmated" or offering teachings and discussion groups centered on helping "poor, maladjusted, lonely" single people with their problems. Singleness was treated as a deadly disease, curable only by matrimony.

I once received a call from an elder of a local church, and the conversation revealed that he felt this way. "Look," he told me, "I have a woman in my church—a former missionary—and, well, I know you meet a lot of singles in your ministry. Maybe you've met someone she might get along with." He was doing what he thought was right. I understood that. But I also knew that, by his actions, he was telling her she wasn't a full person just because she wasn't married.

"All you're feeding her with that kind of thinking," I told him, "is the same kind of feeling she already has about herself: that she's a useless nobody unless somebody comes along and carries her off."

I've heard this kind of thinking referred to as "Knight in Shining Armor Syndrome." It says a person is not complete until someone on horseback comes riding over the mountain, sweeps her off her feet, and carries her off to the Land of Wholeness.

Many singles have "Knight in Shining Armor Syndrome." They walk around feeling as though they are only half a person—almost visualizing themselves with half a body or half a brain—until they find the other half that will make them complete.

They feel like half an Oreo cookie—the one *without* the cream—in search of their other half. Without the other half, they believe they're, at best, a crumbly chocolate wafer of no distinction—definitely not a complete Oreo, in any case.

This feeling of inadequacy feeds yet a second assumption— that all their problems stem from singleness. *If I'm lonely, it's because I'm single. If I lack purpose or direction, it's because I'm single. If I'm emotionally unstable, it's because I'm single. If I'm sexually frustrated and unfulfilled, it's because I'm single.*

Faced with these feelings—and the negative counsel of family, friends, and church alike—all singles want to do is escape. So they fall into a hard, driving search to find Mister or Miss Right. They bend, twist, manipulate, and run to this function or that rally, all in an effort to bring their "curse" of singleness to an end.

> Don't live your life in a "holding pattern," afraid to make any move until your lifetime partner comes along!

But, after a while, the search becomes a snare. Single adults who get caught in the "gotta get a guy/gotta get

17

a girl" syndrome wake up one morning to find themselves living in limbo. They're afraid to make a move for fear that it might keep them from meeting that mythical someone.

Consequently, they make no permanent plans, set no long-term goals, and hesitate to make any life-changing decisions because they're still waiting for the "right person" to come along.

I knew a single guy, a very prosperous man, who was caught in that kind of trap. He had a good job, made excellent money, and lived in a beautiful, modern apartment complex.

One day, I went to visit him at his home and was amazed by what I saw. This affluent and successful man's place was still furnished with old, hand-me-down furniture—Salvation Army, Early Crate. I asked him why he hadn't bought new things. Money wasn't a problem. "I thought about doing that once," he said, "but, well, what if the future Miss Right doesn't like the furniture I buy?"

This man was living his life in a holding pattern, afraid to make any move until his lifetime partner came along. When she did, he thought, she would give him a vision for his life. She would fit him into the mold designed for him. She would set him on the "right track." Then, he could get on with living.

> To God, your singleness is a rare opportunity to grow in your relationship with Him and serve Him without distraction.

But by living like this, he was actually holding himself back from experiencing the joy and fulfillment he so earnestly sought. By rejecting his singleness and longing for the supposedly greener grass of married life, he was missing out on the great things God wanted to do with him—and through him—in this hour. Thus, he felt empty, lonely, and purposeless.

Many single people struggle with the same issues and the same feelings. They, too, live in a kind of twilight zone, waiting for

Mister or Miss Right to rescue them from their plight. They, too, look to marriage as some kind of fairyland where all their dreams will come true. They, too, believe their singleness is some kind of curse on their lives, signifying their own lack of worth and ability to contribute in any substantial way to those around them. And, like the man I just told you about, they, too, are robbed daily of the very things they seek—fulfillment, happiness, and joy.

God doesn't see your singleness as a curse. Neither does He see you as a worthless nobody, ready for the junk pile. To Him, you are a person of promise, ability, talent, and skill who, formed and empowered by Him, can accomplish great things for His kingdom. To Him, your season of singleness provides a rare opportunity for you to grow in relationship with Him and serve Him 100 percent, without distraction. It is a time for knowing and serving Him in a way that is uniquely possible for singles.

I believe God would like you to know six things about your singleness—six biblical understandings of this special season of your life—that will enable you to embrace this new fellowship with your Lord and help you to be all you can be for Him—right now. The next six chapters in this book will examine each of those things in turn. Come with me. Let's explore.

Transitional Thought

PF Flyers and the "Half Person Syndrome"

When I was a young boy, there were some sneakers on the market that were the most amazing set of athletic footwear ever created—or so the makers said. They were called PF Flyers.

PF Flyers were better than any other sneakers around: better than their contemporaries because they had an "action wedge" that the manufacturers claimed could make you "run faster and jump higher."

The commercial for these sneakers was absolutely incredible. It showed a kid running down the street like lightning, leaping over tall fences in a single bound. The kid with the PF Flyers was Superkid, and, from my nonathletic stance as a long, lanky six-year-old, those shoes looked like the gateway to the Promised Land. *If I had PF Flyers*, I told myself, *I wouldn't be a wimp anymore. I'd be able to do all the things I wanted to do and do them better than anyone else on my block or, better yet, the whole school district.*

How I longed for those PF Flyers! I knew if I could just sink my feet into them, all the dreams and plans for my life would come true. Then I'd really be complete and able to get on with the business of living!

My heart was so set on having those shoes that pleaded with my mother practically every day to get me a pair. "Please, Mom. *Please!* Get me a pair of PF Flyers."

"Sneakers are sneakers," my mother would reply, and, time after time, she'd come home from the department store with ordinary, run-of-the-mill sneakers in her hand. They were "nice," but they were never PF Flyers. PF Flyers had that special *action wedge*.

I remember how I used to feel as I slipped my feet into those ordinary, new sneakers. It was real torment for me. I put them on and laced them up, but somehow there was something missing. No matter how nice they looked or what kind of gizmo the manufacturers included in the box (like a Green Hornet secret decoder ring), I was never happy. They weren't PF Flyers, so they weren't anything.

Finally—Real *PF Flyers!*

Then, one day, my mom finally did it. She brought home a pair of the mighty action wedge sneakers. I could almost feel the power in the box as I held it in my hands for the first time. I could almost hear the low hum of energy waiting to be unleashed. Carefully, I opened the box, pulled out the shoes, gingerly put them on my feet, and began walking softly around the house. I didn't want to accidentally kick that action wedge into gear and suddenly find myself zooming uncontrollably up my bedroom wall.

Slowly, deliberately, I walked out to the sidewalk in front of my house. I looked both ways up and down the block, making sure there were no other kids around to trample or cars to crash into. I sure didn't know how long it would take to stop once I took off. Then, I cleared away boxes, trash cans, bicycles, and anything I thought might be in my way. Finally, I was ready for takeoff.

I wasn't sure how the action wedge really worked, but I figured it must have something to do with running. I thought that if you ran as hard as you possibly could, somewhere along the line, when you were at the complete edge of your own abilities, the action wedge would kick in and off you'd go, leaping over walls and careening around street corners to the amazement of everyone on your block. So, I poised myself like a racer at the corner, looked once more for safety, and began to run. Faster and faster I travelled, puffing and pushing my legs as hard and as quickly as they could go. I must've gone a clear city block before I petered out.

What happened? I wondered, confused, as I walked back to the other end of the block. *I must've done something wrong. There must be some other way to get these things to work. Maybe you need to run as fast as you can and then jump at the end.* So, I set myself up at the end of the block, poised myself again, and began running once more. At the end of the block, I took a huge jump. Nothing happened.

After trying a few more times, I gave up. You never saw a more depressed little kid than I was on that day. Mom had been right. Sneakers were, after all, just sneakers.

Taken Captive by a Vain Philosophy

Boy, those commercials sure sold me a bill of goods. I bought every last bit of what they were saying. I believed a vain philosophy. The apostle Paul had something to say in warning about ideas such as those that commercial promoted. In Colossians 2:8–10, he wrote:

> *See to it that no one takes you captive through philosophy and empty deception, according to the tradition of men, according to the elementary principles of the world, rather than according to Christ. For in Him all the fullness of Deity dwells in bodily form, **and in Him you have been made complete**.*
>
> (emphasis added)

The philosophy being sold to singles today, not only by the world but by family and church, as well, is that you're nobody until somebody loves you. Many singles have bought this idea, and, as a result, they place all their hopes and dreams in tomorrow, unable to participate in and fully enjoy today. In the same way that I found no joy in my new, ordinary sneakers, these singles find no purpose or meaning in the situations and people they come in contact with every day. Because of this, life becomes stale and unfulfilling, a string of listless hours of pointless existence. Time spent at work becomes a treadmill of duty. Relationships with friends lack a certain depth and care because real involvement is reserved for a fantasy relationship down the road. Church activity grinds to a halt or consists only of service in which he or she might meet "him" or "her."

Certainly, this is not the way God intends your singleness to be spent. He wants it to be a time full of active service during which you might give yourself totally to Him, committed 100 percent to knowing Him and responding to His call.

How can you begin to do that? By realizing that you're not a nobody because you're not married. You're not half a person, waiting for your "better half" to come along. "On the contrary!" says Paul. In Christ, *"you have been made complete"* (Colossians 2:10).

Today, right now, you have the ability to serve God. He has given you talents and skills that He has designed from the foundation of the world to be used for the furtherance of His kingdom and for spreading the gospel here on earth. Don't be ensnared by the philosophy of the world. Begin living for God today!

STUDY **1** GUIDE

Questions for Knowing and Growing

16 | 1. How do many singles feel about their singleness?

▶ 2. Do these feelings correspond to your own stance? How are they similar? How are they different? What circumstances, input, or people have contributed to your current view?

16 | 3. Who often reinforces negative concepts about singleness?

▶ 4. List some specific elements of society that might contribute to this negative attitude. What message do they give to singles? How is this message perpetuated among singles around you?

16 | 5. Where do many churches and para-church ministries seem to think that ultimate fulfillment comes from?

16 | 6. How do they, as a result, view singleness and approach their ministry to single adults?

▶ 7. What are some problems you can see in such an approach? How do you think such viewpoints can be altered?

17 | 8. What is "Knight in Shining Armor Syndrome"?

17 | 9. How does it affect those singles who succumb to it?

▶ 10. Have you ever experienced this syndrome? Are you experiencing it now? What kind of effect did it (or does it) have on your life as a single? List some ways you might help yourself or someone else break out of such life-stinting, unproductive thinking.

18 | 11. On page 18, we met a single man who lives with old hand-me-down furniture because he's afraid to purchase new ones more to his liking for fear "she" won't like them. What happens to him because of this attitude?

▶ 12. Do you see any of these things happening to you? How have they come about? List some steps you might take to change them.

19 | 13. Mike says many singles feel like this man and gives some common manifestations that reveal it. List them.

19 | 14. How, in contrast, does God view you as a single person?

▶ 15. How does God's view compare with the way you see yourself? What kind of things might you change in order to align yourself more closely with God's purpose for your singleness?

Doing the Word

1. Do some fresh research on the single adult phenomenon. Get acquainted with what's being done today to minister to single adults.

   • How does this line up with what you've learned in this chapter?

   • In what ways does what's being offered either help or hinder singles from laying hold of God's purpose for their singleness?

   • How does this help you discern some things that you individually, as a single person, need to have to grow in your purpose in God? How might what you've learned help you expand and make more relevant the ministry to singles in your own church or community?

   • How might you reach out to unchurched singles in your area and meet their needs through the gospel?

2. Develop a personal plan for getting the most out of your singleness, based on what you've learned about its purpose from this chapter. Include ways you might spend more time with God, develop and use current talents and abilities, and enhance your understanding of your singleness. Make note of any conferences, workshops, classes, or ministry opportunities that would help you grow, and plan to attend them.

3. List again the primary characteristics of a person suffering from "Knight in Shining Armor Syndrome." Organize a biblically based process through which this person might gain freedom from such fear-induced behavior and discover his or her potential for service in Christ.

COMPLETE IN CHRIST

You are a complete person apart from any romantic relationship you will ever have.

T HAT'S RIGHT. THE PERSON YOU ARE TODAY, WITH ALL your abilities and talents, callings and desires, is a full person in the kingdom of God. You are capable of doing great things for Him—not sometime down the road, but *right now*—in the town where you live, in the church you attend, and among the people whose lives you touch.

No romantic relationship, however permanent, will ever make you more satisfied, more complete, or more ready than you are today to serve Christ. You are a complete, whole person whom God is interested in using now for kingdom purposes.

"But that can't be. I certainly don't *feel* like a whole person," you may say. "My life is in shambles. I'm lonely. I'm sexually frustrated. I'm confused. I feel unsettled and directionless. Surely, if I were married, everything would be better. I wouldn't be lonely anymore. I wouldn't have any more struggles with my sex drive. I'd feel whole, and I'd have a real purpose for my life."

But that's simply not true. If you haven't dealt with the cause of your loneliness before you get married, it isn't going to evaporate after you say "I do." If you haven't found purity in your struggles with sexuality as a single person, marriage isn't going to make you pure. If you don't feel complete as a single person, being married to another person isn't going to give you an immediate sense of wholeness or purpose, either.

Why? Because the problems you're dealing with aren't caused by your singleness. Just one look at some of the marriages around you will give you evidence that what I'm saying is true.

Some of the loneliest people I know are *married* people. They're married, yes, but in every real way they are very much alone. Each night they lie in bed next to someone with whom they cannot communicate. In that utter darkness, with tears streaming down their cheeks, they experience the worst kind of loneliness any person can know. As I once heard someone say, real loneliness consists not in being alone, but in being with the wrong person in the suffocating darkness of a room in which no deep communication is possible.

How true and how pervasive that is. Loneliness is obviously not a product of singleness. In fact, it's not confined to singles in any way. You see, whether a person is married or single, only a wholehearted relationship with Christ can meet the emotional and spiritual needs that if left unmet, lead to loneliness.

Forbidden Attractions

Sexual temptation will not be quenched just by getting married either. Take a look at the facts. In almost any newspaper, you can find listings for pornographic movies. On city streets, you'll find people selling their own flesh. On any number of magazine racks, you'll see X-rated material available for purchase.

Do you think only single people watch those movies? Do you think only singles read *Playboy*? Do you think only singles get involved with prostitutes?

What about all the sexual crimes you hear about in the news? Do you think only single people commit them? What about the struggle with promiscuity or masturbation? Do you think only single people have these problems?

Of course not. Just as many married people struggle with sexual problems, go to pornographic movies, visit with prostitutes, and read perverted magazines. Being married doesn't instantly solve the problem.

Why? Because what attracts people to these sinful pleasures is not the sin itself but the idea that it is stolen. They enjoy the forbidden. In Proverbs 9, *"the woman Folly"* says, *"Stolen water is sweet; and bread eaten in secret is pleasant"* (verse 17). Have you developed a taste for stolen water? Does the idea of taking something forbidden attract you?

Take a look at the sexual sin you're struggling with now. Something about it lures you. Is it just the pleasure of the act, or is the pleasure somehow rooted in the forbidden? I believe that if you'll look closely enough, you'll discover the latter is true. Sex has taken on an outer coating of the forbidden. While you're involved in it, your spirit man is very aware that it's wrong. But you've developed such a taste for the forbidden that you can't seem to resist it. It draws you in, pulls you under, and devours you.

> Your desire for the forbidden won't go away when you get married. You have to deal with your desires *now*.

Many people think that once they get married, their desire for the forbidden will go away. They believe their struggles against sexual sin should end because they can now have sex righteously within marriage. But that's not what happens. Because the righteous relationship of marriage does not satisfy people's taste for the forbidden, they're left struggling with the same old temptations as before. They lust after the forbidden. It's the forbidden they really want.

That's why your struggles with sexual sin aren't going to go away the minute you get married. That's why you'll still be tempted and fall prey to the lure of illicit sex and pornographic movies, magazines, and books. That's why you'll struggle with unfaithfulness, even though you really love your spouse. You've got a taste for stolen water. If this desire is not dealt with before marriage, it may end up ruining an otherwise promising relationship.

If you have a desire for the forbidden, you have to deal with that desire *now*. You have to lay it at the feet of Jesus and let it die. Let it die now, so you may live.

"But, Mike, how is that possible? I mean, I *really* struggle with this problem. All I need to do is start thinking about something, and pretty soon I'm doing it. I don't want to do it, but somehow I end up doing it anyway."

That's your first mistake. You *think* about it. You allow that sinful thought to run through your brain over and over again until it finally causes you to sin. That's right—*causes* you to sin. You see, the thought itself isn't a sin. That's temptation. It becomes sin only when you do something about it.

Many people don't know that, though. Wrong thoughts come into their heads, and they immediately think they've fallen. *How could a Christian think like that? That's so sinful*, they think. Then, they just give in.

> The thought itself isn't a sin. That's temptation. It only becomes sin when you do something about it.

Listen. You've got to recognize something here: in this life, you're going to be tempted. Every day, wrong thoughts are going to float through your mind. The problem comes when you nurse those tempting thoughts and let them germinate in your heart until they cause you to sin.

Take the example of Eve and the serpent. The serpent tempted Eve, but it was she who allowed the temptation to fester in her heart and finally cause her to sin. Let's read the account Genesis:

Now the serpent was more crafty than any beast of the field which the LORD God had made. And he said to the woman, "Indeed, has God said, 'You shall not eat from any tree of the garden'?" And the woman said to the serpent, "From the fruit of the trees of the garden we may eat; but from the fruit of the tree which is in the middle of the garden, God has said, 'You shall not eat from it or touch it, lest you die.'" And the serpent said to the woman, "You surely shall not die! For God knows that in the day you eat from it your eyes will be opened, and you will be like God, knowing good and evil." When the woman saw that the tree was good for food, and that it was a delight to the eyes, and that the tree was desirable to make one wise, she took from its fruit and ate; and she gave also to her husband with her, and he ate. (Genesis 3:1–6)

There they were, the fatal words of temptation: *"For God knows that in the day you eat from it your eyes will be opened, and you will be like God, knowing good and evil."* What a lure! It prompted Eve to have bad thoughts about the Lord and to lust for godhood.

But Eve hadn't done anything wrong yet. These were just thoughts, transmitted to her from the adversary. The problem came when she allowed herself to meditate on those thoughts and to consider, for herself, whether or not to eat the fruit of that tree. By allowing herself to be seduced by those thoughts rather than allowing God's command to do battle against temptation, she fell into sin.

In the same way, Satan will tempt you today. He will drop ungodly thoughts into your mind, saying things like, "Go ahead. See that movie. Who will know? Go ahead. Take a look at that magazine. What harm could it do? Go ahead. Give in to that sexual desire. You're only human." That will happen. In this life, it's guaranteed. But it's what you *do* with those thoughts that will determine the outcome.

When the first seed of a thought of sexual sin comes into your heart, don't allow it to take a foothold. Don't sit there contemplating the idea. Don't even meditate on how wrong it is to be thinking that way. Just come back at that thought, full force, with the Word of God. That's what Jesus did when Satan tempted Him.

> *Then Jesus was led up by the Spirit into the wilderness to be tempted by the devil. And after He had fasted forty days and forty nights, He then became hungry. And the tempter came and said to Him, "If You are the Son of God, command that these stones become bread." But He answered and said, "It is written, 'Man shall not live on bread alone, but on every word that proceeds out of the mouth of God.'" Then the devil took Him into the holy city; and he had Him stand on the pinnacle of the temple, and said to Him, "If You are the Son of God throw Yourself down; for it is written, 'He will give His angels charge concerning You'; and 'On their hands they will bear you up, lest you strike your foot against a stone.'" Jesus said to him, "On the other hand, it is written, 'You shall not put the Lord your God to the test.'" Again, the devil took Him to a very high mountain, and showed Him all the kingdoms of the world, and their glory; and he said to Him, "All these things will I give You, if You fall down and worship me." Then Jesus said to him, "Begone, Satan! For it is written, 'You shall worship the Lord your God, and serve Him only.'" Then the devil left Him; and behold, angels came and began to minister to Him.* (Matthew 4:1–11)

The temptations in this passage were real for Jesus. First of all, after forty days and forty nights, you can be sure He was very hungry.

Second, since His trust in His Father was so faultless and complete, you can be sure He was tempted to step out on that word of protection from Psalm 91.

Third, who more than Jesus wanted to ransom the world and bring it back into fellowship with the Father? It was His purpose in coming. Surely, this was His deepest desire. Yet, to succumb to any one of these temptations meant to submit to Satan and fall into sin.

How did Jesus do battle? He used the Word of God. He brought the Word to bear against the area of temptation—time after time after time—until the devil was defeated.

You need to do the same thing. Memorize some scripture verses pertaining to your area of weakness—ones that show God's strength on your behalf and counteract the thoughts of the enemy. Then, every time an ungodly thought comes into your mind, come against it with those verses. There will be a struggle. There was for Christ Himself. But remember: *"Greater is He who is in you than he who is in the world"* (1 John 4:4). You will have victory...in Jesus and by the Word.

One Plus One Equals One

Another thing that needs to be tackled and tossed out of your life as a Christian single person is this myth: marriage will make you complete.

No way. Marriage will not make you complete. There isn't a person in the whole world who can do that for you. If you feel like half a person now as a single, you won't feel any different just because you get married. As a matter of fact, if you get married while you're still feeling like half a person, you'll try to draw your sense of wholeness from your partner, and this impossible demand puts strain on any relationship.

No human relationship—no matter how intimate, no matter how vital, no matter how enriching—can provide ultimate fulfillment for you. Ultimate fulfillment comes from a deeper relationship with Jesus Christ.

35

"Now wait," you may say. "Doesn't God say in His Word that *'the two shall become one'* (Ephesians 5:31)? Doesn't that mean that one-half plus one-half equals one? Doesn't that mean God wants to complete me with another person?"

No. I don't believe that's what God is saying here at all. Where would the miracle be in God bringing two half-people together and making them one person? Besides, in romantic relationships, one-half plus one-half does not equal one whole. If you bring two half-people together, all you'll get are two insecure, dependent people struggling to draw from one another what they should only be getting from the Lord. That's a sad situation, and many bad marriages have been built on that shaky ground.

> In romantic relationships, one-half plus one-half does not equal one whole: it's two insecure, dependent people struggling to draw from one another what they should be getting from the Lord.

The real miracle disclosed in this verse is that God takes two whole, distinct, fulfilled individuals—blessed with their own unique talents and abilities—and makes them one new person together. Now *that's* a miracle.

But God doesn't advocate looking for someone to complete you. He says, "Look to Me as your completion, and the rest will follow." Paul said,

> *So, brethren, in whatever station or state or condition of life each one was when he was called, let him continue there, with and close to God....Are you bound to a wife? Do not seek to be free. Are you free from a wife? Do not seek a wife.*
>
> (1 Corinthians 7:24, 27 AMP)

God is calling you to be content in Him first. He is calling you to look to Him in your loneliness, in your sexual struggles, and in your feelings of rejection and hurt. He is calling you to be complete in Him.

"But Mike, Proverbs 18:22 says that '*He who finds a wife finds a good thing.*' How am I supposed to find a wife (or husband) if I don't look for one?"

Good point. At least on the surface, this verse does seem to indicate the value of searching for a mate, doesn't it? There's just one problem, though. That word *find* in Hebrew doesn't mean "to find by searching for." It means "to discover along the way." This verse is saying, "If you're wrapped up with the Lord, submitting to Him and serving Him according to His will, and along comes someone who ends up being your mate, that's a good thing."

"But what if I do that and God leaves me single? What if I allow myself to be happy and fulfilled as a single person? Won't God look down and say, 'Oh, so he's *happy* being single. Well, I'll leave him that way'?"

That's the risk many singles feel they're taking. They're petrified of being truly happy singles because they think God will look down, see they're happy, and believe they don't need to get married.

Because of this fear, they drag themselves around day by day, refusing to get anything out of the single life. And all the while, they're looking up to God, saying, "See, God? See? I'm miserable. See? I'm one of those who really *needs* to be married. I really *need* that thing in my life. Please." And they use all their energy to make themselves miserable rather than taking their time as single people and using it for the glory of God.

But if you use your singleness simply as a waiting period for Mister or Miss Right, you're not really getting the most out of life as God intended. You're allowing yourself to live in a twilight zone, a no man's land without vision, purpose, or meaning. And people without purpose, vision, or meaning are bound to be discouraged, defeated, and depressed. They're bound to feel worthless. They're bound to live in a world of past rejections and failures. They're bound to feel lifeless and unfulfilled.

Why? Because they are. They've allowed themselves to be caught in limbo, waiting for Mister or Miss Right rather than using their singleness to glorify God.

Let me tell you something: it's in giving your life in service to God and others that the fulfillment, purpose, and joy you seek will come to you. Only when you're willing to give yourself 100 percent to the Lord will you truly begin to live. And only when you're willing to submit to the Lord in this wholehearted way will you achieve the kind of balance that can bring the mate of God's own choosing into your life.

Pushing the Panic Button

Some single people do give themselves wholeheartedly in service to the Lord. They lay their desire for marriage upon the altar before God and start serving Him completely.

Then, one day, a particular birthday rolls around. They reach twenty-five, thirty, thirty-five—whatever age they thought they should be married by—and find themselves still single.

Immediately, they push the panic button. *Oh, no. Oh, no. I'm not married. I'm going to end up old and lonely. I'm never going to have kids. I'm never going to have the kind of relationship I always wanted. The pickings are getting slim now, too. Soon I'll be too old.* And they launch into a frantic search for a partner. They don't care what the person looks like, how they feel about anything, or what they do for a living. They don't have to be Mister or Miss Right anymore. Any *marginally acceptable* person will do.

A woman at one of the singles conferences my ministry conducts said that people in her church call that the "Bride of

Frankenstein Syndrome." You know the story. It involves a scientist who pumps bolts of electricity into dead bodies in an attempt to bring them back to life.

In the same way, she said, single people who have "Bride of Frankenstein Syndrome" drag unlikely, spiritually dead people into church, present them to their pastor, and say, "Pastor, pump some life into this person, please!"

But when you do something like this—dig around in the dirt for somebody, anybody, to marry you—you never know what you'll come up with. And chances are good you'll end up married to someone who doesn't share your vision for service.

I've known people like this. They wanted to be married more than anything else in the world, so they made that their first priority in life. Oh, they wanted to serve the Lord, but, like so many other singles, they felt they needed to get married first. "God, I want to serve You. But let me get married first. Then, we'll take care of the rest of it." So, they accomplished their goal: they found partners and got married. But then, too late, they realized their spouses didn't share the same visions for service that they did. Their mates became weights holding them back from the things God wanted to do with their lives rather than the catalysts for service they had hoped their mates would be.

By putting marriage ahead of God's design for their lives, they ended up married to people who didn't fit into God's plans for them.

Now, God can and will use a relationship like that because, as the Bible says, all things to work together for good. (See Romans 8:28.) But that person should have waited, allowed himself to be led by God, and moved into the service He had prepared for him. Then, marriage, if it were to come along, would have grown out of that service and been in keeping with God's perfect will for his life. Also, it would have allowed him to be used by God, as a single

39

person, rather than causing him to fritter away months and months of time pursuing someone—anyone—to marry him.

So it's important, on several levels, to realize that you are a complete person right *now* in the kingdom of God.

It's important because, in knowing this, you'll be able to begin serving Christ—right now—in your church and community.

It's important because it will give you a right understanding of marriage—not as a cure-all for what ails you, but as a calling of God and a miracle of life, drawing two complete people together as one new person and joining them in common service to the Lord.

> You are a complete person right *now* in the kingdom of God.

It's important because it will cause you to recognize the true source of healing, completion, and fulfillment in your life: the Lord Jesus Christ.

Knowing these three things will help you keep balance in your relationship with God, in your Christian walk, and in your relationships with others (and yourself).

I remember the time God taught me these principles. While in Bible school, I was dating a lovely girl. Everything seemed perfect between us. She was a Christian, and so was I. We both loved the Lord and seemed very much in love with each other.

I dreamt about this girl all the time. I imagined the home we would have together...the white picket fence, the flowers in the yard, and the children. My dreams filled up all my time when we were apart, and I thought a lot about the day I would finally ask her to marry me.

Then, one day, out of the blue, just before school recessed for the summer, she told me we were through. Just like that. No explanation.

I tried to talk to her to find out what went wrong, but I couldn't make any headway. School closed, and we went home.

It was hard going into the summer like that. I couldn't stop thinking about her, and I couldn't stop crying. I grieved day and night. Sometimes I would stare for hours at the silent phone. A few times I even picked up the receiver and dialed the first few digits of her number, but hung up.

Everything seemed to remind me of her—of us—and of what I had lost. Even on my way home from church on Sundays, she was in my thoughts. I would look at the happy families and feel the pain of knowing it could never be so with us. The emptiness in the seat next to mine was as big as the empty feeling in my heart. I was devastated.

At the time, I was ministering in a church a few miles from home. As I drove back from services each Sunday, I passed an ice cream stand. Usually a few pretty girls stood outside talking and eating. Even though I was sure most of them weren't Christians, my loneliness made me long to get to know them.

For several weeks I didn't do much besides stare as I drove by. I thought about stopping and even rehearsed some of the lines I would say. But I never got up the courage to do anything.

Then, one Sunday, I finally became determined. *This time*, I thought, *I feel really ready to talk to someone.* So, I buzzed into the parking lot with my little Volkswagen—VWs were really "in" back then—pushed open the door, and strolled casually up to the counter. Strategically, I placed myself a few feet from one of the cutest girls in the place. I was all ready to make my approach.

Suddenly, behind me, I heard a high, thin voice calling my name. Turning around, I saw a little old lady from the church running over to say hello. I was mortified. What if this woman had seen me...*in action*?

41

I wish I could say that ended my attempts at the ice cream stand, but it didn't. I tried the same thing a couple more times, but each time I ran into somebody I knew. Finally, I resigned myself to a summer alone...with *the Lord.*

As God would have it, I got an apartment that summer next door to a Christian couple. The woman and I became friends. Since this woman was married, there was no question in my mind about dating her. She was just a nice Christian person to fellowship with.

This meant I had to learn to relate to her as a human being. That was a new idea for me. For as long as I could remember, there were only two ways to relate to women: the first as my mother, the second as my date. But this was different from either of those. This was my sister in the Lord.

As the summer progressed and our friendship developed, the Lord revealed to me a rich relationship the likes of which I had never experienced before. It was deep, and it was warm. But it lacked the tension I had felt in dating relationships. I was free to enjoy this person for herself alone, not for some role I was hoping she would play later on.

That same summer, I came upon a book by a monk named Thomas à Kempis titled *The Imitation of Christ.* When I found out who had written it, I thought, *Oh, this is for me. A monk.* (I was really engrossed in living alone and chaste for God that summer.)

That book was the clincher for everything God had been teaching me through my friendship with that married woman. One section remains as fresh in my mind today as it was the first time I read it. It said:

> Whoever intends to come to an inward fixing of his heart upon God and to have the grace of devotion must, with our Savior, Christ, withdraw from the world. No man can safely mingle among people, save he would

gladly be solitary if he could. No man is secure in a high position save he would gladly be a follower. No man can firmly command, save he has gladly learned to obey.

I can still remember how those words hit home. Every word seemed packed with meaning. The sentences stood out as clearly as if someone had outlined them with a yellow highlighter.

I read them one more time, and the Lord began to speak to me: "Until you're free in your heart to be alone, until you're free in your spirit to relate to women just as women—as though you would never marry them—you'll warp your relationships with them."

Suddenly, my mind was flooded with memories of all the girls I had ever dated, and I realized that every one of my relationships with them had been warped. They had been bent out of shape and destroyed by a driving need inside of me to couple off, to marry, to find "her."

I really believed that finding that "certain someone" would make me complete. I believed that all my needs would be met in her. I believed she would make me feel worthwhile and give me purpose and direction. *With her at my side*, I thought, *I could really begin to live.*

But in striving, stretching, and bending to establish those relationships, I had actually ruined them. I couldn't let my relationships be what they were. My girlfriends couldn't be who they were, and I couldn't be who I was. My identity was so wrapped up in theirs that I worried constantly about losing them. I had no personal sense of identity.

But during that summer, God was reshaping my life and redirecting my thoughts. He was taking my eyes off marriage and fixing them on Him instead. He was teaching me that no romantic relationship, no matter how fulfilling and satisfying, could ever give me the completeness, the identity, or the purpose I so hungered for. The only person who could give me that was Jesus Christ.

The Source of Fulfillment

Have you ever yearned for someone so deeply that you've cried yourself to sleep? Have you ever felt completely worthless because you haven't had someone to "go with" like everybody else? Have you ever clung ferociously to a relationship as if it was your very life support?

Well, God is saying to you today what He said to me in Bible school. No romantic relationship can bring you the fulfillment you seek. True fulfillment comes through a deepening relationship with Jesus Christ.

How can you know that kind of fulfillment in your relationship with Jesus? How can you discover what it really means to be complete in Christ? You can begin by seeing Him as your supplier and giving Him first place in your heart. Only when Jesus is first in your life—before your possessions, before your job, before your career, before every relationship, and before marriage—will you truly be fulfilled.

> Only when Jesus is first in your life will you truly be fulfilled.

One single person who grappled with this issue was the rich young ruler mentioned in the gospel of Matthew:

And behold, one came to Him and said, "Teacher, what good thing shall I do that I may obtain eternal life?" And He said to him, "Why are you asking Me about what is good? There is only One who is good; but if you wish to enter into life, keep the commandments." He said to Him, "Which ones?" And Jesus said, "You shall not commit murder; you shall not commit adultery; you shall not steal; you shall not bear false witness; honor your father and mother; and you shall love your neighbor as yourself." The young man said to Him, "All these things I have kept; what am I still lacking?" Jesus said to him, "If you wish to be complete, go and sell your possessions

and give to the poor, and you shall have treasure in heaven;
and come, follow Me." But when the young man heard this
statement, he went away grieved; for he was one who owned
much property. (Matthew 19:16–22)

From childhood, the rich young ruler had observed the Mosaic Law, obeying every jot and tittle. He never murdered anyone or committed adultery. He never lied, cheated, or stole. He always honored his parents and loved his neighbor as himself. I'm telling you, this was one incredible person. I don't think too many people today—born-again, Spirit-filled believers included—could claim as great a record as he did before God.

Even though he had done all those things, he felt empty and incomplete inside. He was still unfulfilled, so, he came to Jesus and asked what he was lacking.

Jesus looked upon the heart of that young gentleman and knew immediately what the problem was. He loved his possessions more than God. So, Jesus said to him, *"If you wish to be complete, go and sell your possessions and give to the poor, and you shall have treasure in heaven; and come, follow Me"* (Matthew 19:21).

But the price was too high for this young man. His possessions meant too much to him, and he went away grieving.

How about you? Where is Jesus in your life? Does He truly have first place in your heart? Or is there something else you love too much to surrender it to Him?

If there is something inside yourself that you would be unwilling to relinquish in order to obey and follow God, you need to deal with that thing *right now.* You need to come before the Lord and ask Him to enable you to give that thing to Him. Whatever it is—be it your desire for marriage, your material possessions, the comfortable home you live in, the church you've become accustomed to, or the job you love—let go of *that thing.* Pour it out before the Lord, and let Him take first place in your heart. Only when you are willing to surrender your dearest desires to God will you be able to know completeness in Jesus Christ.

Jesus wants to be your fulfillment. He wants to be your consolation in time of loneliness. He wants to be your healer when rejection and hurt cause you pain. He wants to be your victor in areas of sexual struggle. He wants to complete you in areas of personal fulfillment. He wants to be your strength, causing you to reach out in boldness on behalf of the gospel and gospel principles in your daily life. But you need to be willing to let Him be all those things for you.

Let Jesus be your fulfillment. Let Him deal with your loneliness and your battle with sexual sin. Let Him give you a purpose and a vision. Let Him use you—a complete person, full of ability, talent, and skill—now for kingdom purposes.

If you're willing—and God is willing to make you willing—He promises you fulfillment beyond your wildest dreams. Matthew 6:33 says, *"But seek first His kingdom and His righteousness; and all these things shall be added to you."*

Allow yourself to find fulfillment in Christ. Put Him first in your life. Let Him take care of everything else. He promises He will. And God doesn't lie. (See Numbers 23:19.)

Transitional Thought

Finding True North

Have you ever had the experience of counting on something and having it fail you? I don't think there are many of us who haven't. Just by the very nature of this world, most things are bound to change. People change, situations change, jobs change, governments change. Even trees, mountains, lakes, and rivers change after a while.

Yet I know plenty of people who stake their lives on these variables and build their houses on shifting sand. Then, when the sand does its shifting, their whole lives are thrown askew because they placed their trust and confidence, their view of themselves, others, and the world, on something that isn't constant.

Perhaps you've seen this happen in your own life. When people at church are patting you on the back, telling you how great you are, you're on a high. But, if several weeks go by and people aren't saying too much, you get depressed. You've based your self-worth on the input of others and, as a result, you're up one day and down the next.

This isn't true only for singles. For example, if my wife looked to me for some kind of security, a definition of who she was and what she was worth, she'd be riding a pretty wild roller coaster, emotionally speaking. Yes, there are days when I wake up and feel like I can conquer the world and nothing I experience in the next twenty-four hours can discourage, defeat, or take me by storm; but there are also days when I'm in the pits and God seems very far away. I'm empty, dry, and lacking in confidence. If my wife based her own self-concept on mine, she'd be full of joy and confidence one day but depressed and anxious the next.

The same is true for people who base their self-image on what they own. Take the guy who invests $140,000 in a spanking new, fire-engine red Porsche, for example. Why would *anyone* buy a car for $140,000? There's really only one reason: because it makes him feel like *somebody*.

Let's face it: when you drive down the road in your Porsche with your fancy scarf trailing behind you in the breeze and your leather-gloved hands firmly in charge of that steering wheel, you feel like a million bucks. And of course it doesn't hurt when the guys and ladies begin to "ooh" and "ahh," either. You're worth something. You're *somebody*—somebody with a *Porsche*!

But what happens when, one day, your car is parked at the local shopping mall and a hyperactive, freckle-faced kid bounds out of the station wagon next to you and slams his door full force into your shining new body work? All of a sudden, you're no longer the big shot, fancy Dan with the hot set of wheels. You're just a guy with a dented car that people stare at, not out of admiration but criticism: "Boy, if I had a car like that, I'd never let *that* happen to it." You've gone from a blazing success to a simpering failure, all in one little dent.

Without God, It's a Roller-Coaster World

That's the way life is when you base your self-concept on things and people. Like the old song says, "I'm flying high in April; shot down in May." It's just proof positive that you can't guide your life by things that change. You need something you can count on, something constant.

Navigators realize how essential it is to have something immovable they can count on to keep their direction straight. They know they can't depend on land because if they move out of sight of it, it's no more use to them. They can't depend on other boats, either. Even if those boats were to stay consistently the same distance away from each other and from you, that's no guarantee that all of you wouldn't drift one hundred feet west together.

Ancient seafarers had to find something more reliable, something that would always be in the same place all the time. That's why they turned, in the Northern Hemisphere, at least, to the North Star. Seamen know that the North Star will always be in the same place and, because of that, they can keep their direction straight by seeing where they are in respect to the star.

Our North Star: Jesus Christ

As Christians, we have a North Star: Jesus Christ. We know that no matter what happens, either *to* us or *around* us, we can turn to Him and know where we are by the guidance of His Word. He is *"the same yesterday and today and forever"* (Hebrews 13:8 NIV).

When I have Jesus Christ as my focus, I no longer need to compare myself to others. Jesus does away with that because it's no longer others who determine my sense of worth but Christ Himself, and in Christ I know I'm okay.

Centering on Jesus also lets me know that, no matter what ups and downs may occur in my life, no matter how many cracks I see in my personality, I always have value. I am His creation, formed perfectly for the service God had planned for me from the foundation of the world.

No man or woman, no matter how startlingly beautiful to the eyes, challenging to the wit, or compassionate to the heart, can ever offer you this kind of security. That stability comes from only one source: Jesus Christ. He is the One who never changes.

STUDY **2** GUIDE

Questions for Knowing and Growing

Part One: Marriage Is Not a Cure-all

29 1. What does Mike have to say about romantic relationships and completeness in your adult life?

29 2. What does he say about the person that you are today?

▶ 3. How does this compare with your own view of romantic relationships? Do you agree or disagree with his viewpoint? Why do you hold that view?

29-30 4. What is his comment to those who attribute their struggles with loneliness, sexual frustration, and lack of purpose to being single?

30   5. What definition does Mike use for "true loneliness"?

▶ 6. How do you feel about this definition? Do you agree with it? Why or why not?

31   7. Why will sexual temptation not be quenched by marriage, according to Mike?

31   8. What verse of Scripture is used to illustrate this point?

▶ 9. Are there other reasons singles struggle with sexual sin? List them and suggest some ways to deal with the problem. Use Scripture to support your conclusions.

32   10. What is the first mistake many people make in fighting ingrained, habitual sins such as sexual immorality?

32   11. What does meditating on sin do to you?

32-33 12. What is the scriptural illustration Mike uses to show how meditation upon sin works to defeat the Christian?

33 ► 13. What illustration from Scripture does Mike use to show you how the process works? What insights does it give you in dealing with habitual sins of your own?

33-34 14. How should we deal with that temptation when it comes our way?

34 15. What passage of Scripture does Mike use to illustrate his point?

34-35 16. What three battle techniques does the passage reveal?

35 17. What is the verse of Scripture he gives as encouragement in the fight?

► 18. Identify some problems in your life for which you have blamed your singleness. Are those things you list truly confined to the single experience? What can you do to cope more adequately with the challenges you face?

Part Two: "Two Halves Make One Whole" and Other Myths

36   1. Many singles quote the verse *"the two shall become one"* (Matthew 19:5) as a passage that indicates a person isn't whole until he marries. What does Mike say about this passage?

▶ 2. How does this view affect your visions of marriage and singleness?

37   3. Some singles have suggested that Proverbs 18:22, *"He who finds a wife finds a good thing,"* indicates the need to search for a mate. What does Mike say?

▶ 4. How does this challenge or support your view of finding a mate?

37-38   5. What does Mike say is the danger inherent in using your singleness as only a "waiting period for Mister or Miss Right"?

▶ 6. Have you seen this evidenced in your own life or in the lives of others? What kind of action might you take to free yourself from this type of "on hold" lifestyle?

| 38 | | 7. How does Mike say singles can truly find the fulfillment, purpose, and joy they seek?

▶ 8. List some ways you have put your life "on hold," waiting for your spouse to come along. What things can you do today to become free from these habits and become more alive for Christ?

| 39 | 9. What is the "Bride of Frankenstein Syndrome"?

| 39 | 10. What often happens to people who marry someone they've found while suffering from this condition?

▶ 11. Have you ever had "Bride of Frankenstein Syndrome" or known someone who did? What seemed to cause it? If this person acted on his or her feelings, what was the result? Suggest some ways to deal with and overcome that panicky feeling.

| 40 | | 12. Why does Mike say it's important to realize you are a complete person right now in the kingdom of God? Cite the three reasons.

▶ 13. List some things you've used, other than a relationship with Jesus Christ, to help you find completeness. What made you think these things would help? What do these thoughts reveal about your needs as a single person? How can a right relationship with Jesus Christ help meet those needs?

▶ 14. In this chapter, Mike shares a story from his own life about something that helped him become more comfortable in his singleness. Read the story again. What experiences does it bring to your mind? How do they relate to your own concept of singleness?

42 15. What passage from *The Imitation of Christ* became a turning point in Mike's relationships, especially with women? Write it out.

43 16. What did the Lord say in response to this advice?

43 17. What did this experience cause Mike to realize?

43 18. What happened to his relationships with women because of this situation?

43 | 19. What was God trying to do in Mike's life that summer?

▶ 20. How do the words of Thomas à Kempis affirm your current beliefs or challenge you to change? What steps might you take to enact the changes the passage suggests?

44–45 | ▶ 21. Mike examines the life of the rich young ruler. What did Jesus tell this young man he needed to do in order to be complete?

45–46 | 22. How can you know fulfillment as a single?

46 | 23. What Scripture passage illustrates this point?

▶ 24. Are there things in your life that are keeping you, as they kept the rich young ruler, from being complete? What steps can you take that will help you release them to the Lord?

▶ 25. In the past, what has been your attitude toward romantic relationships? Has this chapter changed your attitude? If so, in what way?

▶ 26. Examine one particular sin that has stubbornly remained in your life. Based on this chapter, what specific action can you take now to do battle when you are tempted to commit this sin again? How will you feel when you are tempted?

▶ 27. In this chapter, Mike discusses a common fear among singles that keeps them from finding joy in that season of their lives: *If God thinks I'm happy being single, He'll leave me that way.* Because of this, many singles elect to stay miserable. Have you ever felt this way? What do you think such fears reveal? What do you think might be the solution? Be practical.

▶ 28. Mike suggests that the path to fulfillment for singles is through giving themselves in service to God and others. Have you found this to be true in your own life? If you have, give a specific example that illustrates it. If not, what obstacles do you find in your life to giving such service? How do you think you can overcome such limitations? What does the Bible say on the subject?

Doing the Word

1. Take a test. For one full weekend (or even a week, if you're daring), give yourself some extended time alone. Allow no distractions. This includes TV and radio. You may read, but only Christian literature. Keep track of your reactions. How do you feel? What does this reveal about yourself? What areas does God point out that He wants you to work on? Make some concrete plans that can help you deal with such feelings in the future.

2. By yourself or in a group, take a book of the Bible (Ephesians or Colossians are good choices) and look up how many times *"in Him"* is mentioned. Examine the context of each instance. What does it say about our lives in Christ? How can you apply it to your life?

GOD'S ULTIMATE WILL

Marriage is not God's ultimate will for your life.

WHAT ARE YOU TALKING ABOUT, MIKE? WHAT DO YOU mean by that? Are you telling me I may never get married? Are you saying I may be single *forever*?"

No, I'm not saying that at all. God is concerned with your marital status. He's concerned with your needs, your desires, and your happiness. He's also concerned with the job that you take, the place where you live, and the people you live with. But none of these is His ultimate will for your life. None of them constitutes His final goal for you. None of them is the ultimate thing He's shooting for.

God's ultimate will for your life is this: to conform you to the image of His Son. (See Romans 8:29.)

God is not concerned with location, education, or any other material thing as much as He is in making you more like Jesus. To God, it's not a question of singleness or marriage, of secular or Christian employment, of living on Main Street, USA, or in Nairobi, Kenya—it's a question of forming you into the image of His Son.

Your heavenly Father is interested in having you understand this truth. He wants you to know that His main purpose is to make you more like Jesus. And whatever it takes to make you more like His Son, God is willing to do—because everyone in the world needs a reflection of Christ in his or her life.

This means that if God believes the rigors of single living will make you more like Christ, He's going to keep your single for however long or short a season He believes is necessary. If He feels the married life—with its own set of challenges, pitfalls, and refinements—will cause you to be more like Christ, then He will bring you into that kind of relationship. The bottom line for God is always the same: He wants to make you into an image of His Son because the world needs people who will be mirrors of God, shining the love, the Word, and the good news of Christ into the hearts of others. He needs Christians—little Christs.

But whatever He chooses, the question for you becomes, *Which do you want more: to be married or to be like Jesus?* Are you allowing God to use your singleness to make you more like Jesus, or is all your energy going into trying to escape the very situation in which God has placed you?

Who will be Lord of your life? Will it be marriage or Jesus Christ?

That is the challenge God is facing you with today. That is the question you must answer. That is the issue you must resolve. Who will be Lord of your life? Will it be marriage or Jesus Christ? Which do you love more?

God is calling you to choose His Son. He's calling you to lay down your life for Him, marital status and all. God wants you to love Him more than any other thing in your life, and He's calling you to submit to the shaping force of His Spirit—to embrace your singleness and use it, for however long it lasts, for His glory.

Many singles, however, battle against the dealings of God in their lives. They see the pain of never having married, or of being widowed or divorced, as some horrible curse placed upon them, limiting them from truly living a full and happy life. *If only she hadn't walked out on me. If only I were married. If only that relationship had lasted. If only my spouse hadn't died on me. Then, I'd be a stronger person in God.* They see their experiences as obstacles when they really should see them as stepping stones—purifying agents designed to strengthen them and make them more like Jesus.

Perhaps you're a single parent. It's not easy to raise children by yourself. But if you will allow Him to, God wants to use the stress and stretching of single parenting to make you more like Jesus.

Perhaps you're divorced, with no children. Being alone after such a painful experience is a big adjustment. You've got a lot of difficult emotions to deal with, and many times, as a Christian, you can't find other Christians who know how to respond to your situation. I make no attempt to justify their behavior. We in the church have a long way to go in learning how to minister to the divorced. But neither do I advocate you to take a "poor me" stance that closes you off from allowing God to use this experience to make you more like Him.

In Jesus Christ you have a Friend, Scripture says, *"who sticks closer than a brother"* (Proverbs 18:24). In Jesus Christ you have One, Isaiah 53:3 says, who is *"acquainted with grief."* In Jesus Christ, you have One who has experienced rejection and betrayal by those He loved. In Jesus Christ, you have the healing and power to overcome pain and be shaped by your life today into a stronger and clearer reflection of Him.

If you've never been married, the same applies to you. Jesus Himself was a single adult. From every indication, so was the apostle Paul. Isaac, too, was single into his forties. But singleness never prevented them from being used by God. In fact, Paul recommended the single life as one that brought him closer to the Lord.

God wants to use your singleness to bring you closer to Him. He wants you to begin to come to Him with every need you have. When you're lonely, when you're depressed, when you're experiencing temptation, or when you're looking for purpose and meaning in your life, He wants your first response to be seeking Him.

If you're widowed, God wants to make your widowhood more than a time to mourn the passing of a mate—more than a time to while away the hours. He wants it to be a time of growth and service in Him. If you will let Him, He will use the rigors of widowhood to do just that, and to conform you, day by day, into a clearer reflection of His Son.

Whatever type of single person you are, your decision remains the same. You can look at all the things that are happening in your life as problems to be removed or escaped, or you can see them as God does—as a refiner's fire meant to strengthen and purify you, step by step, into the image of His Son.

When you choose Jesus, you choose life. When you choose Jesus, you choose freedom. When you choose Jesus—the author and finisher of your faith—and follow Him, conforming yourself to His image, you don't need to get worked up about geography, location, education, or position anymore. At that point, wherever He puts you down will be a good place because you're going to be growing in Him. You're going to be formed into the image of God's Son.

How does God refine you into the image of His Son? By allowing the heat of circumstance to come to bear upon your life.

In both the Old and New Testaments, we see God reflected as a refiner and a purifier. Take, for example, Proverbs 17:3: "*The refining pot is for silver and the furnace for gold, but the Lord tests hearts.*"

Do you find yourself reading that verse, shaking your head, and thinking, *Now, what does that mean, "the Lord tests hearts"? Is God going to test me to see if I'll be bad or good?* No. To be honest, God knows what you're made of. He knows that it's quite likely you will fail. He knows your every weakness and doesn't have to put you to a test to discover them.

The testing referred to in this passage is the kind that is used to make gold pure. In its raw form, gold has a lot of impurities running through it that mar its appearance. So, in order to get them out and make the gold as fine and pure as possible, it is put into a crucible and heated with intense fire. Under those conditions, the gold liquefies, and the impurities within it rise to the top, appearing as tiny flecks on the surface. A worker then takes a fan or bellows and blows the flecks off the gold's surface.

As more heat is applied, still more flecks surface and again are blown to the side. Finally, the worker takes a scoop and removes whatever impurities remain. In the end, the surface of the metal is mirrorlike in purity, and the refiner's face is perfectly reflected.

In the same way, God uses the heat of circumstance to purify you. He lets the stresses and strains of single living touch you so the impurities in your life can rise to the surface and be blown away by the Holy Spirit. Then, you will more perfectly reflect the image of His Son to the world.

Trial by Fire

A few years ago, I bought a new car—not a "new" used car but a totally new, "never-owned-by-anyone-but-the-bank-and-me" car.

I was proud of that car. I thought I'd never own one that still had that new smell to it. I grew up in a poor home, and my mom didn't even own a car. We went everywhere by public transport or on foot. So, the day I bought my brand-new car, I was bursting inside with excitement.

Well, one weekend after we brought the car home, I was outside our apartment putting a new, customized stereo tape deck in the dash. As I was crouched along the front seat working away, I heard my little son, then three years old, come tearing across the graveled lot to greet me. In one of his hands was a fistful of little stones.

As he got closer to the car, he began to skid a little. Watching this happen, I grew more tense every second. Then, what I most feared happened. He collided into my car, stone-filled hand first, and scraped a little of the paint off my lovely, steel-blue import.

"Toby!" I yelled hysterically. "Look at my car. Oh, my car! My car!" I was almost weeping with rage. "Get in the house!" I screamed. "Get in the house! Go on. *Now!*"

My son just stood there, frozen on the spot in fear. His knees trembled, and he sniffed. Tiny tears rolled down his cheeks.

"Did you hear me? Get in that house, now!" Sobbing now, his eyes and face red from the tears, that little three-year-old whom I love so dearly ran down the walk and into our home.

I stood there for a second while the shock of what had happened waned slowly from my body. Gradually, I began to come back to my senses. *How could I have screamed so much at my own sweet, little three-year-old over an inanimate piece of metal, chrome, and rubber?*, I thought. But I had. In that moment I realized how much that car really meant to me. It meant more to me, obviously, than my own sweet son.

> God allows bad situations to come into your life so that you will be purified and ultimately become bread to feed a hungry world.

Now, if you had asked me before that incident about the worth of that car, I would have said, "The car means nothing to me. God can take it any time He wants to." But then God sent a little ambassador to me and said, "I want some of the paint from your car," and what happened? I exploded.

In order to help me become a stronger Christian, God used the heat of that circumstance to cause the sinful attitude inside me to rise to the surface so it could be dealt with and blown away.

In the same way, God will allow the circumstances in your life to purify you. He'll let them heat up to such an intense degree that the dross inside of you comes to the surface. Then, when it is exposed, He'll blow across it with His Spirit. In the end, you'll be stronger and purer, a clearer reflection of Christ to the world.

The Master's Threshing Floor

God has another way of refining you and making you more like Jesus. It's called *winnowing*. John the Baptist said this of Christ:

> *And His winnowing fork is in His hand, and He will thoroughly clean His threshing floor; and He will gather His wheat into the barn, but He will burn up the chaff with unquenchable fire.* (Matthew 3:12)

A winnowing fork is an instrument a farmer uses to process raw wheat into a substance that can finally be used to make bread.

The farmer takes wheat from the field and lays it down on what is called a threshing floor. He beats the wheat with sticks, stomps on it with his feet, and rolls over it with logs, shaking, stretching, and flattening it out. Next, he takes his winnowing fork and throws the wheat into the air. As the wheat is tossed, a wind blows through it, separating the precious wheat from the chaff.

Have you been feeling as though you're beaten down, rolled over with the logs of life, and stomped on? Have broken relationships and negative emotional experiences left you shaken, uprooted, and beaten down? Do you feel as though nothing is tied down in your life? If you're on shaky ground, it's an unsettling feeling. But I want you to know that if you respond rightly to these situations, you're going to grow in God and become more conformed to the image of His Son.

God has allowed these situations to come into your life so you may be purified and ultimately become bread to feed a hungry world. He's allowed you to experience the rigors of single living. He's allowed you to go through the pain of separation and rejection.

He's allowed it so that you might be more closely conformed to the image of His Son.

But many singles don't understand the dealings that God brings into their lives. "Why would God allow that divorce to go through if He really loved me?" "Why would He let my husband die?" "Why would He let me experience that abusive relationship?" "Why would He allow me to be alone and lonely?" "Why would He allow my engagement to be broken off?" Then, despondent, discouraged, and even angry at God, they run away from those situations rather than allowing them to help them be conformed to the image of His Son, as He intended.

Following are five forms of testing the Lord uses to purify and strengthen you to make you more like Christ. I believe that by understanding them, you will be better able to respond to them in a fruitful way and grow—as God intends you to—into a purer reflection of Christ.

1. The Wilderness Test

Have you ever been in a place with the Lord where you were stretched to your human limit? Your kids were having some mega-sized problems involving school friends. Your job was requiring more of you than you had to give. Yet as you looked at your life, you knew you had been obedient to God insofar as you knew His will for you. So, why the struggle? Why did He let it go so far? Why did He allow you to get to the end of your proverbial rope?

The answer, I believe, can be found in God's dealings with the children of Israel in the wilderness. Soon after they were freed by Pharaoh, the Israelites were led through the Red Sea. They watched as God provided a way of escape for them and destroyed their enemies in the process. So far, so good. But what was on the other side of that sea waiting for them? The wilderness—a vast expanse of dry, arid land where water and food were difficult, if not downright impossible, to find.

66

It didn't take long for the Israelites to begin reminiscing about "the good old days" back in captivity when they always had enough to eat and drink. "We had it good back there," they began to grumble. "Now, since we've obeyed God, look at the problem we're in. We followed Him. We did what He told us to do. And now we're hungry and thirsty."

Why would God do a thing like that to the Israelites? It doesn't seem to make a whole lot of sense. Why drag thousands of people out of a land where they were oppressed but fed, only to bring them to a place of drought and starvation? *To teach them dependence on Him.* God's servant Moses explained it like this:

> *And He humbled you and let you be hungry, and fed you with manna which you did not know, nor did your fathers know, that He might make you understand that man does not live by bread alone, but man lives by everything that proceeds out of the mouth of the LORD.* (Deuteronomy 8:3)

Out in the wilderness, the Israelites could do nothing humanly to survive. This forced them to call upon the Lord. When they did, they saw miracles happen. Manna fell from the sky to feed them, and water sprang from a rock to quench their thirst.

Victory in life does not come from anyone but God.

God was teaching them to lean upon Him for their sustenance and to rely on Him for their nourishment and strength. He was teaching them, quite literally, that even when they could accomplish nothing in a situation, God could come through for them. He was teaching them that victory in their lives did not come from them but from Him alone.

Why did God want them to know that? Because He wanted them to be able to respond rightly when He brought them into the Promised Land. He wanted them to know it was He, and He alone, who provided; and He knew that if they didn't learn this principle *before* they received their blessings, their chances of backsliding were great, if not guaranteed. That's why, in that same chapter, Moses warned,

> *Beware lest you forget the LORD your God by not keeping His commandments and His ordinances and His statutes which I am commanding you today; lest, when you have eaten and are satisfied, and have built good houses and lived in them, and when your herds and your flocks multiply, and your silver and gold multiply, and all that you have multiplies, then your heart becomes proud, and you forget the LORD your God who brought you out from the land of Egypt, out of the house of slavery.* (Deuteronomy 8:11–14)

God wanted the Israelites to depend on Him, not on themselves. He wanted them to know beyond a shadow of a doubt that it was not their strength or ability that won them the Promised Land, but God and God alone.

As you follow the Lord, He will bring you into your own wilderness. You will be faced with a situation—perhaps in your home, with your family, on the job, or at church. God will speak a word to you, and you will step out in faith, only to find your human resources are not enough to help you survive. You won't have the talent, the ability, or the finances. You'll be up against the wall. If God doesn't bail you out, you will just wither away.

God will bring you to that place for a purpose. He wants to teach you to rely on Him. He wants to teach you to call upon Him. He wants you to realize that He is your provider.

Particularly as a single person, you have a unique opportunity to see the fruit of this kind of testing. As a single person, you have a tendency to depend on yourself. Without a spouse, you shoulder a lot of responsibilities. You have to see that the bills are paid. You have to see that the kids are clothed and given schooling and health care. You have to see that they're given spiritual teaching and guidance. Even without kids, the responsibilities are still shouldered by only one person—you. You have to make sure the car is registered, inspected, and repaired. No one will be there to remind you. You have to see to it that you're adequately nourished. You have to make sure the rent is paid. *All* of it is your responsibility.

Because of this, it's easy, even without meaning to, to depend on yourself without allowing God to move on your behalf and show He can be trusted to provide.

Sooner or later, you will reach the end of your rope. Perhaps you're thinking to yourself, *Mike, I've already reached that point. I'm there now. I might even be a little bit beyond it. I've gotten to the point where I'm just barely scraping by, day by day. It's agonizing.*

I want you to know that God has brought you to this point for a purpose. He wants you to stop trusting in the arm of the flesh and begin trusting in Him. He wants you to recognize that your whole life—from your spiritual walk to the food on your table—depends upon Him.

God has brought you to this place of need so you may call upon Him and find Him faithful to provide. God has brought you to this place of loneliness so you may find comfort and wholeness in Him. God has brought you to this point of sexual weakness so you may find strength to overcome in Him. God has brought you to this point of frustration in dealing with your children so you may find words of counsel, compassion, forgiveness, and correction in Him. God has brought you to this point of discouragement and frustration in your job so you may find

> God has allowed you to be single now so you may find your fulfillment—not in another human being, but in Him, its only true source.

encouragement, wisdom, and strength to persevere in Him. God has allowed you to be single now so you may find your fulfillment— not in another human being, but in Him, its only true source.

In the wilderness, you learn to depend on God—even in the most dire circumstances. In doing so, you find strength for your life and put yourself on solid ground with Him. Then, when the blessings come—and God promises they will—you will know they are from the Lord, not yourself.

2. The Test of Total Commitment

You can't go very far in the Christian walk without experiencing the purifying process.

Another type of testing God uses to purify us is the "Test of Total Commitment." In this test, God challenges us to lay down everything we have and follow Him.

Have you ever been in a situation in which God asked you to give up something you loved very much? Did He ever put His finger down on one area of your life and say, "Surrender that thing to Me"? If you've been a Christian for any period of time, I'm sure God has done that. You can't go very far in your Christian walk without experiencing this purifying process. Just giving your life to Christ involves this kind of test. You must choose between your sinful life and the Christian walk.

But as we walk further down the road with Christ, the refining process continues. God has a call upon our lives. He wants to hold first place in our hearts. So, every time something exalts itself above Him—every time there's something inside us that spars with God for our attention—He'll ask us to give that thing to Him.

With Abraham, it was his only son, Isaac. With the rich young ruler, it was his material possessions. With you, it may be different. Perhaps, for you, it's a relationship. That's a common—and major—one for singles. Perhaps it's your right to control your children's destiny. Perhaps it's your right to have a comfortable place to live. But whatever it is, it causes you to be double-minded in your pursuit of God. You want to follow God, yes. But there's something else you desire, as well—something you're not willing to relinquish.

The problem is that if you don't let go of it, it will keep you from being fulfilled as a child of God and from growing in Him. It will prevent you from being formed any further into the image of His Son. It may even cause you to backslide.

I knew a young woman whom God used powerfully—especially among single people. Head of a vibrant, successful singles ministry at her local church, she had spoken at several of our earlier retreats.

Not long ago, I called this woman's church to see if she would speak at another conference. The pastor got on the phone. "Mike, she's not coming to church here anymore." I was stunned by the news. "Not going to church there? What do you mean? Six months ago—"

"Well, not anymore," he said, and he began to unravel a sad tale to me. "It began with a man she met at work. He was not a Christian, but she began developing a relationship with him, anyway. At first, I said nothing. I knew she understood that she should not be unequally yoked with an unbeliever, and I hoped the relationship would wind down without my input. Unfortunately, it didn't."

Weeks turned into months, and still no sign of a breakup was in sight. The pastor's concern grew. This woman was not only endangering herself but giving a wrong kind of witness to the singles she led. He knew he had to confront her.

A few days later, they met in his office. "I've noticed you're seeing this man," he began as delicately as he could. "And I know

71

he's not a Christian. As for you, you're a singles leader. You know you shouldn't be seeing this person. In fact, I was hoping you'd stop seeing him on your own, but you haven't. Now I feel I have to ask you—and this is very hard for me to do—to break off your relationship with him or to step down...."

One mention of discontinuing the relationship was enough to set her off. "This man is better than any Christian man I have ever met," she said, almost becoming livid. "So, if you're saying I can't lead the singles ministry anymore if I continue to see him, then I guess I won't be involved in the ministry anymore." And from that day on, she wasn't.

For a while, she kept coming to services on Sundays, but, gradually, that stopped, too. "For all I know," the pastor said with a sigh, "she's fallen away from Christ by now and has backslidden."

"What happened to her?" I wondered aloud. "How could someone so on fire for God fall away so quickly and so finally?"

"I guess," the pastor said, "she never really yielded her right to marriage to the Lord."

In this woman's life was a desire for marriage that countered her desire for God. It was a strong desire, but one she kept buried, for the most part, in the deepest recesses of her heart. There, deep within her, that desire took root and grew until one day it was too big to keep buried. It surged to the surface and took control, claiming first place in her heart.

Then, when she was confronted with a decision, she chose her relationship with that man over her relationship with Jesus Christ.

That's the chance you take when you continue to covet something strongly and are not willing to relinquish it to God. Just the fact that you have trouble releasing it to Him shows you the power it holds on your life and the place it has in your heart. *It's more important to you than God Himself.*

God knows the danger of having a desire like that in your heart. He knows that, when the pressure is on, this desire inside you could cause you to fall away from Him. So, God calls upon you—gently but persistently—to yield that thing to Him. Oh, you can put it off, but every time you try to go forward in God, that same issue will come to the surface—maybe not at first, but eventually. God will point to it patiently and say, as He did to Abraham, "Take your one, your only, and offer it to Me." It's the Test of Total Commitment, which, when submitted to, will open the door to massive growth in your Christian life.

3. The Old Enemy Test

Have you ever seen the transforming power of God operate in the life of an unbeliever with, by human standards, really horrible problems and sin—a drug addict, a prostitute, or perhaps a drunk? One minute, he's the vilest person you've ever met, and the next, having accepted Jesus as his Lord and Savior, he's made completely pure without even a foul word coming out of his mouth. His life has been radically changed. In an instant, he's been made holy.

That's an amazing and exciting thing to witness. But have you ever wondered why the power of God is able to do that for him, yet you're left struggling with sins that beat you down day after day after day? God has given you that same power. Why does this person experience such immediate victory while you are left doing battle with some sins for years and years?

I've certainly been puzzled about this before. I'd look at my life and see certain besetting sins that, no matter how hard I tried to resist them, just refused to die in my life. I'd look at them, then at what God had done for others, and say, "Lord, if You can clean up people like that in an instant, why are these things still in my life? Why don't You just take care of them? Why don't You just take them away?"

Then, one day, I was reading the book of Judges, and I came across this passage in chapter 3:

> Now these are the nations which the LORD left, to test Israel by them (that is, all who had not experienced any of the wars of Canaan; only in order that the generations of the sons of Israel might be taught war, those who had not experienced it formerly). (verses 1–2)

The passage nearly jumped off the page at me. Immediately, I began to see God's purpose in allowing me to struggle with those besetting sins. He wanted me to learn to do battle with them so I could become strong and victorious in Him. He wanted me to "*be taught war* [as I] *had not experienced it formerly.*"

> God wants you to learn how to do battle with sins so that you can become strong and victorious in Him.

You are probably struggling with certain things in your life. Perhaps they are sexual desires; perhaps a fear of relationships; perhaps a habit of smoking or eating too much; perhaps the habit of thinking negatively all the time. You've fought with that thing so many times that you're almost ready to quit. In fact, there have been times when you've given in. *That's it. I quit. You win. Walk over me.* You've gotten up and been beaten down by that thing so many times that you just can't live with the battle anymore.

You've prayed many times that it would go away. *If I could just get rid of this thing,* you've thought, *I could really do something for God.* But the truth is that God left that thing in your life so you *could* do something for God. You see, it's in doing battle, learning to war with the old enemies in your life, and—in God—finding victory over them that you'll become strong and perform exploits for God. It's in learning how to conquer a debilitating fear, a strong sexual urge, or a tendency to fly off in anger that you'll be purified and strengthened in God. You'll learn how to fight. You'll learn how to conquer.

God has places for you to conquer. Did you know that? He has places for you to rule and reign over beyond your imagination. God has said we will sit with Him in heavenly places and claim the whole of creation for Him.

I believe that is what heaven is all about. I believe that eternity is not going to be spent sitting around strumming harps. I believe we're going to rule the earth in Jesus' name. (See Revelation 5:10.) We're going to go forth to do battle for our Lord and bring everything under His dominion.

But He can't do it with a lot of wimps. He needs people who have learned war. He needs people trained for battle, willing to persevere against even the toughest foes. That's why He's allowing you to go through the Old Enemy Test right now. That's why He's allowing the struggles of your singleness to remain—so that you can learn to wrestle, fight, do battle, and conquer in the power of your Lord, Jesus Christ.

Are you struggling today with some besetting sin or weakness? Don't be ashamed. That battleground is your place of training. You're being trained to fight the good fight so you can reign with Him in heavenly places.

4. Test of the Unfulfilled Word of the Lord

Has God ever spoken a word into your life, but you've never seen its fulfillment? Perhaps you felt the call to be a leader in your local church. Perhaps God was speaking to you about becoming a pastor, an evangelist, a prophet, or a teacher. Perhaps He was giving you visions of leadership in the business community, in social services, or in a creative field. As God unfolded His plan before you, you became excited.

But now, the months and the years have gone by, and nothing seems to have happened. You're sure the Lord spoke to you, for undeniable recognition resounded in your heart. Yet, everything in your life seems to indicate that this particular vision will never come to pass. You're still sitting in the pew of that big congregation and setting up chairs on Sunday. You're still just another cog in the wheel at your firm. You're still typing letters rather than being at the helm of that publication God has laid on your heart. You're still serving coffee in the church basement rather than speaking the Word in front of the congregation as God said you would. Perhaps you've begun the journey only to experience a series of frustrations and failures. Maybe the doors have been slammed in your face over and over again. You see no indication that God's vision is going to come to pass.

Joseph would understand what you are going through. God gave Him a big vision, too. He said his own brothers would bow down before him. The Lord told Joseph he would be a leader of his people. Yet here he was, a little shepherd boy who was thrown into a well by his brothers, sold into slavery, and finally thrown into jail. He suffered one discouragement after another. Why? What was happening? Psalm 105:16–19 describes the situation:

> And He called for a famine upon the land; He broke the whole staff of bread. He sent a man before them, Joseph, who was sold as a slave. They afflicted his feet with fetters, He himself was laid in irons; until the time that his word came to pass, the word of the LORD tested him.

God spoke a word into Joseph's heart that Joseph knew was true. Even when his brothers grew angry, threw him in a hole, and sold him into slavery, he knew. Even when he was falsely accused of attempted rape by Potiphar's wife and thrown in jail, he knew. Even when the prisoners he had helped didn't remember to intercede for his freedom, he knew. Despite all the circumstances that spoke messages to the contrary, Joseph believed God, and it acted as a refiner in his life, purifying and strengthening him in his walk with God.

Imagine yourself in Joseph's place. God has given you a vision: your brothers are going to bow down to you. Then, what happens? Your brothers throw you in a hole and stand over it, looking in at you. You have two choices at this point. You can get discouraged and allow doubt and unbelief to creep in. *This isn't the way God said it would be. Maybe I heard Him wrong. Maybe He didn't give me that vision, after all.* Or you can proceed in faith, standing on the Word. As Smith Wigglesworth said, "God said it. I believe it. That settles it."

What happens when you choose to walk in faith? All the thoughts, feelings, and attitudes that try to come against that stance are forced to fall away. You become purified and strengthened in your faith, and your eyes are more firmly focused on the Lord and what He wants to accomplish in you.

> When you choose to walk in faith, all the thoughts, feelings, and attitudes that try to undermine your confidence will fall away.

Then, imagine yourself as Potiphar's right-hand man. Everything's going well. You're the boss's favorite. He can count on you. You've earned his trust by serving him with excellence and doing every task, however large or small, to the best of your ability. Then, one day, his wife begins to pursue you in an unwholesome way. You don't want to transgress the trust placed in you by your boss, and, being a Christian, you certainly don't want to offend God. So, you avoid her. But she keeps it up, pursuing you whenever she gets the chance. Finally, when she sees you're not going to give in, she gets mad and decides to get revenge. She tells Potiphar you tried to rape her, and he throws you in jail. Not only are you a slave, but you're an imprisoned one.

Again, you've got two choices. You can become embittered: *How could she lie about me? How could Potiphar believe her? It isn't fair. It isn't right.* Or you can do what Joseph did: submit to the situation, continue to believe God, and become the best prisoner you can be so that God will be glorified.

Since Joseph chose to submit, the circumstances he faced were able to purify him. He was able to learn humility and servanthood and be available to help others, even in the most dire circumstances. His eyes were focused all the more on the Lord, and he was trained in faith amid all circumstances. Even in what could have been the deepest, darkest, most discouraging moments of his life, Joseph grew in God and bore fruit.

In the same way, God will allow you to be tested as you wait for the fulfillment of His word to you. Yes, at times, you will look around and the vision will seem anything but near. But if you will submit to each situation you find yourself in—if you will yield to God those circumstances that could be frustrating, depressing, discouraging, even defeating, and believe His Word in the midst of them—God will use them to purify and strengthen you, making you more like His Son day by day.

5. The Test of No Sense of the Presence of God

Do you know what it is to be left alone by God? Do you know how it feels to come into a service where the power of God is moving and feel absolutely nothing at all? People all around you are getting stirred by the pastor's message. You can see it in their eyes. Afterward, many are talking about the sermon. But there is no response inside of you. You feel nothing, even though you know you should. The message has left you dead.

This happened to me when I was in Bible school. I lost the conscious sense of the presence of God. I went to chapel services every day, sang hymns, and listened to sermons. Afterward, the whole student body would be buzzing about what they had gotten out of the service. Not me. I would go in, sing, and listen. But I received nothing. The hymns didn't stir me, and the words of the sermon didn't speak to my heart. I felt nothing at all. I was dry. This really bothered me. God had given me a call to preach, and here I was, not even stirred by the Word. I hoped it would change and that the fire would return. But it didn't. The weeks rolled by, and I remained unmoved.

Finally, Christmas break arrived. I felt I had to make a decision. *God surely doesn't want preachers like me,* I thought. *Not people this deadened, dried out, and unresponsive to His Word.* So, I decided to go home for the holidays and never come back.

Well, I went home and went to church, not because I wanted to, but because I felt it was my duty and obligation to do so. I remember how everyone ran up to greet me. "How is Bible school?" they asked enthusiastically. (Everyone thinks Bible school is heaven on earth.) I didn't know what to say. How could I tell them what I was feeling? How could I say I felt nothing at all? How could I tell them I was thinking of quitting school altogether? I didn't want to be sour, so I just made some noncommittal statement, like, "Oh, yeah, well, really, it's never been like this before," and basically kept my mouth shut.

During the holidays, our church had a special speaker come to minister. She was an extremely gifted woman, sensitive to the movement of the Spirit. Everyone got excited and planned to attend. But within me there was only hesitancy. I had heard much about this woman's ministry and how she spoke to people's innermost needs, but I feared that even this would leave me dry. *What if I go and still don't sense the presence of God?* I thought.

Yet, despite my feelings and fears, I decided to go. I listened as she spoke to the congregation. The words were right in accordance with Scripture. People around me were stirred by the message, but nothing happened to me. God, as far as I could tell, was nowhere to be found.

After her message, some people went forward for prayer. I watched as she prayed with them. Some even had tears in their eyes as she prayed. How I longed for God to touch me like that. It had happened to me before, but it seemed like such a long time ago. I stood to leave, and as I did, the visiting minister caught my eye and waved me forward with her hand.

Oh, no. She wants to pray with me. Oh, no. I'm going to be exposed. Now she'll know how dead I am. It'll be so noticeable. Reluctantly, I moved toward her. Then, she began to pray: "You have prayed, and it has seemed to you as though the heavens were brass. You have cried out to God, and you have said, 'Come to me. Help me. Come to me where I am!' But God cannot come to you where you are. *You* have to come to Him. If He met you where you were, you would stay there; you wouldn't move on. So, He, as your loving Father, has held Himself back from you. He has shut His ears to your cries that you might long for Him and go forward in Him. And now He calls you to come to Him."

> Don't settle down when you reach a place of spiritual comfort; God will keep moving, and you will be left behind.

Tears rolled down my checks as she spoke. For the first time in months, I could feel His presence, and I knew the words she spoke were important ones for me. Even as I had heard them, I realized what had gone wrong in my relationship with God. I had created a place of comfort for myself. Reaching a certain plateau of spiritual experience, I had settled down. I felt so good there, so at ease. Everything was so right. But while I sat in that place of comfort, God left. He moved on.

Let me tell you, nobody plans on losing God. I sure didn't. Neither did Mary and Joseph. When they left the feast at Jerusalem, they didn't look around for Jesus. They just assumed He was with their group somewhere.

That's the way we are sometimes, too. We set up a little place of security, start doing something in our church, get involved in our own little projects, and *assume* He's there with us all along. But He's not. He leaves.

A few years ago, an uncomfortable incident happened to me while I was shopping for clothes with my son, Toby, who was then three years old. Like all little kids, Toby liked to play in the clothes racks whenever we went shopping. He'd hide himself in those racks and walk around, getting his head inside all the clothes.

One day, we were out together, and I was looking for some pants. As usual, Toby was in the racks of clothing. From time to time, I would look down, find him, and tell him to get out. Well, as often happens when you're absorbed in clothes shopping, I got caught up examining some pairs of pants to see how well they were made, whether I thought the color was something I liked, what they cost, and so on. After looking at a few pairs but finding nothing I wanted, I decided to leave the store.

I called to my son. "Okay, Toby. We're ready to go. Come on." No answer. "Toby, come on. We're going now." Still no reply. I listened for a rustle of clothes in one of the nearby racks. Nothing. Slowly, I began walking up and down the aisles, lifting up clothes, parting hangers, and discreetly calling his name. There was no sign of him anywhere.

"Toby," I said, a little louder. "Toby." I was getting tense now but still trying to cover it. "Excuse me," I said, tapping a mild-looking, middle-aged lady on the shoulder. "Uh, have you seen a little boy? He's about *so* high. Blond hair. Little red shirt, blue pants?" I looked up. "Toby! Toby!" My pitch was getting higher now. By this time, I had searched the whole department. He was nowhere to be found. "God, where is he?"

I picked up my pace and began jogging around the store, screaming his name. I didn't care what I looked like now. All I wanted to do was find my little boy. "Toby! *Toby!*"

I ran up to a customer service desk, my eyes bulging with anxiety. "Have you seen a little boy?"

"You'll find him....You'll find him," the lady behind the desk said quietly, trying to reassure me. By this time people were running all over the store.

Suddenly, out of the mall entrance came a woman. She had my son by the hand, and she was looking at me as if to say, *You call yourself a parent?* I felt bad, but I was so glad to see my son that I almost didn't care. "Oh, my son, my son. You found him. Oh, thank you, thank you, thank you. Toby, my son, my son. I'm so glad to see you." Then, a little sternly, "Don't *ever* do that again. Stay near your father."

Now, I never went into that store intending to lose my son, but I did. Similarly, nobody intends to lose God. But they do. They get involved in something and get ready to go when, all of a sudden, they realize He's not there.

At first, they try to remain calm. "God...hello, God. I know You're there. God?" But there's no answer. We try again. "God, I'm calling to You. Come here, God. Come here." Still no reply. Then, we panic. "Jesus...why isn't it like it used to be? Where *are* You? Why aren't You here? Please, come back. Please come here."

But He can't come to you. Like a loving father, He's holding Himself back so He can call you to Himself.

Today, if you're in a place where you can't sense God as you used to, He is calling you to come to Him. Don't stay where you are. Don't say it has to be your way. Don't ask Him to meet you where you are. Go to Him. Follow Him, and keep your eyes on Him. That's what He's trying to teach you. He's trying to show you the importance of following Him as Christ did and of hearing and responding to His call.

Perhaps you've been looking at the testings of God in your own life as you've been reading this. Maybe you haven't been feeling His presence. Maybe you've been feeling tossed in the air, without roots. Perhaps you've been struggling with the same old problems that have plagued you for years. You may have been asked to surrender something and follow Him. Or perhaps you're struggling with an unfulfilled word.

But I want you to know something. These testings have come for a purpose—not to cause you to faint or give up, but to form you into the image of Jesus Christ, the Son of God.

If you will allow them, these testings can be more than trials endured. They can be stepping-stones of Christian growth, paving the way to make you more productive for Christ.

Transitional Thought

An Unbroken Heart

God uses many circumstances and individuals to shape us more perfectly into the image of His Son. A while back, the singles magazine I edited published a story by a single man who was formed by such pressures through an unrequited love relationship God allowed in his life.

Jonathan Kattenhorn was a wholehearted Christian single who, even though confined to a wheelchair and unable to write without someone else's aid, was actively serving the Lord at a Christian camp in California. During his time there, he met a young woman named Kate. Kate was not handicapped, but she was one of those rare individuals who was able to look beyond physical limitations to the heart of a person and develop a relationship with him based on who he is, not what he looks like.

After the camp closed for the summer, Jon and Kate continued their friendship through letters and phone calls. "I began to wonder where our relationship might be headed," Jon wrote in the article. "I'd steadily dated a handicapped girl once, and we'd even talked about marriage—but we'd broken up. Now, at twenty-five, was I about to find a girlfriend at last?"

Communication between the two was more than steady, and, with the help of others, Jon frequently wrote letters and phoned. "One day," Jon said, "my Dad, who'd noticed all my corresponding and phoning, warned me, 'You'd better slow down or you will ruin your friendship with Kate.' But I didn't listen."

Jon continued to visit Kate whenever he was at the camp for meetings, and they maintained a friendship that was even further cemented since Jon had become, like Kate, involved in special education. He was now teaching agriculture to the handicapped. Then, Jon asked Kate to be his date for the camp banquet and double-date with his parents for lunch before the event. "That sounds like fun," she said, agreeing.

Falling in Love but Keeping His Distance

In the months that followed, Jon tried to maintain an emotional distance inwardly, referring to her as his "big sister" though all the while, inside, he hoped she would one day be his girlfriend. "One night in March," he recalled, "while I was playing my Autoharp, I began to realize I'd been thinking more of Kate than I was of my Lord Jesus Christ. I prayed, asking forgiveness. As I told Kate about it the following day, she said, 'You know, we need to keep our minds on Christ more than on other things.' Through Kate, God was trying to show me that He had to be Lord no matter what happened."

The following summer, Jon returned to the camp where the cook gave him some devastating news. "'I hear Kate has a boyfriend,' she told me. I couldn't figure out how it could be true. *I am Kate's boyfriend*, I thought. I had things all planned out."

But God had other things in mind. "Sitting on my bed, I opened my Bible and hoped for some comforting thoughts. I found Romans 8:28: *'In all things God works for the good of those who love him, who have been called according to his purpose'* (NIV). *But why?* I thought. *There must be some mistake.*"

Jon went to his friend, Bill, for counsel and, having confessed his love for Kate and his desire to see God's best achieved in her life, the two prayed.

The following weeks were fraught with complications. "Kate was willing to see me," Jon wrote, "but every weekend something interfered."

Finally, some weeks later, they were able to get together. "I asked her, 'Is there any more to our relationship than now?' Her answer: 'I don't know; I'm not ready for anyone yet.'"

Kate and Jon continued to correspond and she spoke freely to him about Dick. "Is this a 'Dear John' letter?" he asked her, but she said it was not. "Dick and I are looking for God's will," she told him.

Some months later, Kate and Jon went out to dinner for her birthday. He asked her about Dick. "We have to talk about that," she said. "I didn't have a tape and I wanted to tell you myself. Dick and I are engaged."

Finding Hope amid Dashed Dreams

Jon tried to take it lightheartedly, joking that there could be no more dates since he didn't date married or engaged women, but inside he was hurting. He couldn't understand what was happening. The next day, while reading for a Bible course, he came upon Hebrews 11:39–40: "*And all these, having gained approval through their faith, did not receive what was promised, because God had provided something better for us."* All of a sudden, Jon understood. "God could provide some better thing for me, too."

Kate told Jon she still wanted to be friends, but, at first, Jon wasn't willing. "I fought bitterness," he explained, "but in the end I was happy for Kate. I went to [her] wedding and actually enjoyed it. The ceremony was not the one I had hoped and dreamed about, but I knew it was what God wanted. To my surprise, Kate's marriage was the start of a new and better friendship for us. No more did I have to put on a front around her so that she'd like me. Now I could be 'just Jon.'"

"As I look back over the two years of friendship that followed," Jon wrote, "I would not change one thing about our relationship. Isaiah 55:8–9 expresses what happened: *'For My thoughts are not your thoughts, neither are your ways My ways, declares the LORD. For as the heavens are higher than the earth, so are My ways higher than your ways, and My thoughts than your thoughts.'"*

"I may still be single," Jon says, "but I have a strong friendship with Kate. I'm working on a friendship with Dick, too. Relationships like these are put together by God; He knew from the beginning that I would never be Kate's husband. I'd be a very close friend. Sometimes loving God means trusting Him—for something better."

That same God who had "something better" for Jon has the same thing in store for you. No matter what circumstances come your way or relationships come and go in your life, God's purpose is to achieve His best in you and to cause you to grow in Christlikeness. *"For I know the plans I have for you, declares the LORD... to give you a future and a hope"* (Jeremiah 29:11).

Through the tugs and pulls of every experience, God is shaping you into the image of His Son. That's His ultimate will for your life; in glad submission to the caring Potter's hand, you will find fullness of joy.

S̲t̲u̲d̲y̲ **(3)** G̲u̲i̲d̲e̲

Questions for Knowing and Growing

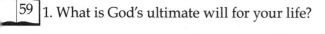

59 | 1. What is God's ultimate will for your life?

50 | 2. What is the question for singles in light of this will?

50-61 | 3. What does Mike say singles normally do when God chooses to deal with them through a season of singleness?

51-62 | 4. How, conversely, does God want to use our singleness, if we let Him?

52 | 5. What happens when you choose Christ over every other situation, circumstance, person, or thing in your life?

87

62   6. How does God refine you into the image of His Son?

62   7. What verse from Scripture does Mike use to support his point?

62-63   8. What does the word "test" mean as it is used in this verse?

63   9. How can the refining of gold be compared to the way God uses the heat of circumstance to purify our lives?

65   10. What is another way God refines us?

66-78   11. Name the five tests of God, as identified by Mike in this chapter.

66-70   12. Define, in your own words, the Wilderness Test. What is its purpose?

68-69   13. Why do singles have a unique opportunity to see the fruit of such testings?

▶ 14. Where have you seen the Wilderness Test operating in your own life? What has happened to you as a result? Be specific.

70-73 | 15. What is the Test of Total Commitment?

▶ 16. Have you seen it in operation in your own life? What happened to you as a result of that test? Be specific.

73-75 | 17. What is the Old Enemy Test?

74 | 18. Where is it illustrated in Scripture?

75 | 19. What is its purpose?

▶ 20. Where have you seen it operating in your own life? What has happened to you as a result of that test?

75 | 21. What are the benefits of learning to do battle?

75 | 22. Why should you not be ashamed of your struggle with sin?

75–78 | 23. What is the Test of the Unfulfilled Word of the Lord?

76 | 24. Where is it evidenced in Scripture?

78 | 25. What is the purpose of this test?

▶ 26. Have you experienced this test in your life? What were the circumstances? What changes came about in you as a result?

78–83 | 27. What is the Test of No Sense of the Presence of God?

83 | 28. What is God's purpose for it?

▶ 29. Have you experienced this test in your own life? What were the circumstances? What changes did it bring about in you?

Doing the Word

1. Do a private Bible study of the word "test." See what other dimensions of understanding you can glean from what you read.

2. Read a biography of a great man or woman of God and examine the illustrations of "testings" this person went through. Note how you can implement his or her responses in your own walk with God. (I recommend *Is That Really You, God?* by Loren Cunningham.)

SINGLENESS DOESN'T MEAN REJECTION

Singleness doesn't mean rejection.

MANY SINGLE PEOPLE LABOR UNDER THE FALSE CONclusion that their status in life is a sign of rejection. They look at their singleness—whether caused by divorce, a broken engagement, or lack of relationships leading to marriage—and see it as a stigma on their life, almost akin to a highly contagious, socially unacceptable disease. *I'm a reject. I'm no good. I'm a nobody. If I were somebody—if there were anything attractive in me—then I'd be married.*

To be honest, many of them, especially those who are divorced or have never been married, can look into their past and point to incidents of deep rejection, times when people made them feel worthless or never even gave them a chance.

But just being rejected does not make a person a "reject," worthless, or some kind of leftover in life.

Singleness is neither a stigma nor a social disease. It's a matter of *choice*. "What?! Mike, how can you say that? I'm divorced. I'm widowed. My fiancée broke off our engagement. I never wanted this lonely life. Not ever. How can you tell me I'm single because I've chosen to be?"

Because it's true. Oh, you may not have become single in the first place because you chose to be. Someone else may have initiated the divorce. Someone else may have broken off the engagement. Someone else may have died. But right now, as you are reading this book, you *are* single by choice. Let me explain.

If you wanted to be married today, you could be. I guarantee that I could find somebody for you. If you had no criteria, no real guidelines, or no moral standards to speak of, I could find someone who'd be willing to marry you. Anybody who has no standards can get married.

But you *do* have standards; and, whether or not the idea is comfortable for you, you're single because of those standards. You've made certain choices in your life. Some of them may have been good, and others may have been bad. That matters little. The fact is, you chose them. You're single by choice.

Even your choice to be a Christian has narrowed the field. As a Christian, you've made a lot of choices that non-Christian singles haven't. You're not of this world, and you don't follow their standards. You've chosen to follow Christ, and it has set you apart. It has limited your choices.

> Singleness is neither a stigma nor a social disease. It's a matter of *choice.*

Let me give you a few examples. You don't go to some of the places that non-Christian singles go. You don't think along the same lines as non-Christian singles. You don't even approach your work and your relationships the way they do. And that's because of a choice you've made. A choice for life—a choice for Jesus Christ.

That's why a lot of you are single today. You're single because of Christ. You're single because you haven't been willing to compromise the truth you stand for. You're single for God. And on the day you stand before Him, He's not going to look at you and rate you on your marital status. He's not going to say, "Oh, poor Janie. Somehow she just never made it to the altar. She just didn't make it." He's going to look into your heart and see the uncompromising stand you took with the desire of being wholly pleasing to Him. He's going to see your singleness not as a failure but as the price you were willing to pay to follow Him.

You've chosen to be single. It's not some evil curse, and it's not a sign that you've failed. If anything, it's a sign that you've chosen Jesus as your Lord and Savior and that you stand for righteousness. That's a fantastic choice, indeed, and a great reason for being single. *You're single for Him!*

But this doesn't mean that you're instantly going to be a whole person, completely repaired and freed from the pain of past rejections and hurts. In fact, the rejections you've suffered can actually keep you from experiencing the full life you can have as a Christian single, redeemed by God.

However, there is a biblical program I'd like to share with you for overcoming the rejections you've suffered and the hurts that keep you from experiencing that full life in Christ. To uncover it, we need to go to the heart of the gospel, in the words of Isaiah:

Who has believed our message? And to whom has the arm of the LORD been revealed? For He grew up before Him like a tender shoot, and like a root out of parched ground; He has no stately form or majesty that we should look upon Him, nor appearance that we should be attracted to Him. He was despised and forsaken of men, a man of sorrows, and acquainted with grief; and like one from whom men hide their face, He was despised, and we did not esteem Him. Surely our griefs He Himself bore, and our sorrows He carried; yet we ourselves esteemed Him stricken, smitten of God, and afflicted. But He was pierced through for our transgressions, He was crushed for our iniquities; the chastening for our well-being fell upon Him, and by His scourging we are healed. All of us like sheep have gone astray, each of us has turned to his own way; but the LORD has caused the iniquity of us all to fall on Him....But the LORD was pleased to crush Him, putting Him to grief.

(Isaiah 53:1–6, 10)

How well we know these verses. They testify of the saving work of Jesus, who died once to free us from sin and restore us to fellowship with the Father. *"He made Him who knew no sin to be sin on our behalf, that we might become the righteousness of God in Him"* (2 Corinthians 5:21). Yes, we understand it well enough; but how often we live as though it had never happened.

How often have you said to yourself, after having done something wrong, "Oh, no. Look what I did. It'll be *days* before I can come into God's presence again," and sentenced yourself to a self-imposed exile from the presence of God? If you're like others, you've done this probably more times than you care to remember. Do you know how that breaks His heart? I do.

Once, when I was the associate pastor of a local church, I got an intense desire to experience God face-to-face. I had read in the Old Testament that Moses had such an experience, so I thought, *How much more should I be able to experience something like that as a New Testament believer?* One day, I began praying to God for such an experience. "Oh God," I prayed, "I want to know You as Moses did. I want to know You face-to-face. Reveal Yourself to me."

As I prayed, the presence of God began to fill the room. It flowed into every corner and grew in intensity. A warm, liquid presence of Him rested everywhere. It was incredible.

Then, in a flash, I realized what had begun to happen. I knew God was about to manifest Himself to me in all His glory, and suddenly I grew afraid. I blurted out, "No! Don't do it!" In a second, the presence was gone, quickly and suddenly.

I sat in my room and wept, conscious of having shut God out. Then, He spoke to me: "Mike, why are you afraid of Me?"

I said, "God, there are some awfully wrong things in my life. It's one thing to talk about seeing You and knowing You in a face-to-face way. But I'm no Moses. I've got some things in my life I'd be ashamed to show You. I'd be ashamed to look into Your face."

Then, God spoke a word to my heart that has affected me ever since. He said, "Michael, your sin already separated Me from Somebody I loved very much. When you turned away, it separated Me twice."

When God allowed His Son to die on the cross for our sins, the act was permanent. From now on, we who are saved never have to be separated from God again. It's why He paid the price. Yet, continually, we live as though that provision were not made. We act as though we must still pay the price. That's very sad because it's already paid in full.

But Jesus bore more than our sins on that day. Isaiah 53 says He bore our hurts and rejections, as well. He took them all on Himself so we could be free.

The Cross Is an Exchange

Because of Jesus, we can exchange our rejections for His acceptance. We can exchange our hurts for His healing, His peace, and His joy. I want to show you how.

The first thing I want to deal with is rejection. I think I'm well acquainted with rejection. Since I grew up in a home without a father, I had to do many things myself that other boys got to do with their dads. If I wanted to take up a sport, for instance, I had to make all my own arrangements. I had no father to sign me up or talk to the appropriate people for me.

One thing I wanted to do badly when I was small was play Little League baseball. I knew tryouts in my home town were coming up, so I managed to get myself a glove and find some neighborhood kids to practice with.

I practiced every chance I got. Wherever kids were playing baseball, you would find me. I was out there with them.

> Because of Jesus, we can exchange our rejections for His acceptance. We can exchange our hurts for His healing, His peace, and His joy.

Finally, the day of tryouts came, and, because we didn't own a car, I had to find another way to get there. So, I walked. It was a long walk—more than two miles. But I wanted to be in Little League more than anything else.

When I arrived at the field, I saw fathers and sons practicing and waiting their turns to try out. All over the diamond, boys were running, catching, and pitching. Being just a boy, I wasn't sure of the procedures, so I got out on the diamond and joined in.

You never saw anyone who put more heart into the tryout than I did. I pitched with all the strength in my little arm. I caught high pops. I fielded. I ran as fast as I could. And all the while, I hoped one of the coaches would notice me. I didn't have a father to point me out: "Hey, did you see that kid catch that high fly ball to center? That's my boy, Mike." I just had to hope my performance would speak for me.

As dusk settled on the ballpark, the coaches took their pads in hand and began reading aloud the names of those who'd made the league. Team after team was called, name after name. I strained to hear my own. I never did.

Perhaps there was some form to sign I didn't know about. Perhaps I had to introduce myself to someone. I don't know. All I do know is that I felt rejected, and the little boy's heart inside me was shattered. Being such a small child, I didn't know how to handle that hurt. So, I just shoved it deep down within my being and went on. Unconsciously, however, I made a decision: I would never go near sports again.

Years later, when I was in high school, that unconscious vow I'd made still remained in effect. I loathed anything to do with sports, but I didn't know why. I'd skip gym class, and I didn't care. Even if they threatened to take me out of school, I still wouldn't go. I just hated anything to do with sports, all because of a wall I had unconsciously built during my childhood.

Although I became a Christian in my senior year of high school, my strong dislike for sports remained. I wouldn't even watch sporting events on television. It was that bad.

Then, one day, more than five years later, circumstances forced me to confront the feelings deep inside. I was associate pastor of a local church at the time, and some of the men from the church decided to start a softball team. They asked me to join. "Come on, Mike. You've got to be a part of it. It's going to be great."

Suddenly, inside of me, a great surge of resistance arose. "No, I don't want to. I just don't like sports. Really." But they insisted, so I gave in. After all, I *was* associate pastor of the church. I *should* get involved, even if it *wasn't* my thing. Reluctantly, I went out, got a mitt, and began practicing my skills again.

On the day of the first game, I felt a little nauseated and nervous inside. It was a weird reaction, and I didn't understand why I felt so strange. I didn't know the wall I had unconsciously built as a child still stood inside me.

Sensing my reluctance and tension, my teammates put me out in right field. If you know anything about right field, you know it's the place the baseball almost never goes. It's where you put the low man on the team.

So, there I was in right field, the tension and anxiety mounting. Then, the game began. Occasionally, a ball would come in my direction and—to my shock and delight—I'd catch it. This happened a few times until, eventually, I began to get excited. Not just a little thrilled, mind you, but way-out excited, beyond comprehension. I didn't understand it. I wasn't doing too much—just catching the ball now and then. But every time I did so, I experienced a surge of emotion. I imagined myself catching a high fly ball. I heard the crowds—all three bleachers of kids and wives—shouting and screaming. It was an inordinate reaction, and I didn't understand it at all. But I knew one thing for sure: I was really *enjoying* myself.

That night, I got home and began to pray. "God, what was that all about? Why did I get so thrilled about such an ordinary thing?" That's when He reminded me about the rejection from Little League many years before. "Mike," God said, "for years you've carried the rejection you suffered as a child in your heart. It's kept you out of every kind of sport and even caused you to keep from watching them or reading about them. But today on that field, for the first time in your life, you were laying the rejection of the past on Me, and you were free."

That was a thrilling moment for me. I realized for the first time what God had done for me through His Son, Jesus Christ. He had shouldered the rejection of my childhood upon Himself so I could find freedom from pain and fullness of joy in my life with Him, right down to an activity as basic as baseball.

Perhaps you've had some deep rejections in your life and, like I did, you've built walls to protect yourself from ever experiencing them again. Some you consciously remember building; others you don't remember. But that matters little. What I want you to know is this: you can be free from that wall today. Right now, you can come out from behind that wall, take the fear of rejection—whether a result of that painful divorce, that broken engagement, or those unfulfilled relationships—and lay it upon Jesus Christ. You can take the rejections of childhood that have caused you to build walls between yourself and others and lay them upon Him now. You can lay everything that has ever held you back or made you feel unlovely upon Him and find healing, freedom, and joy.

Won't you do that *right now*? Take that rejection of your spouse to Jesus. Take that breakup with your fiancée to Jesus. Take the wounds of your childhood to Christ, and lay them upon Him. He will set you free.

Supernatural Release

Another thing Christ bore on the cross for you is *grief* or *sorrow*.

I used to have a habit of laughing at tragic things. For example, if someone told me about a fifteen-car pileup on Route 69, I would picture all these people hanging out their windows ogling the scene while a bunch of others ran around, comically hysterical, like characters out of a Three Stooges film. And I would laugh. It was really strange.

Once, while I was in Bible school, I began telling a rather sad story to a girlfriend of mine. It involved a chick-hatching project I had done in grammar school.

The project required me to keep a close watch over some eggs and make sure they hatched without problem. I took my responsibilities seriously. I watched those eggs vigilantly. When I couldn't be home, I made sure my mother watched them for me. They had to be turned at exact intervals, and I made sure they were—whether I did it or somebody else did it for me.

After a few weeks, the hatching process was almost over. Late one night, after most of the chicks had come out of their shells, I was carefully watching the last unhatched egg. I didn't want the chick to hatch when I wasn't looking because I feared it might burn itself on the heater that kept the incubator warm.

Unfortunately, I grew very tired. Try as hard as I might, I could not keep my eyes open. Eventually, I dozed off, only to be awakened minutes later by a high-pitched peeping sound. It was the last chick. It had hatched and, as I feared, burnt itself on the heater.

As I told the girl the story, I began to recall how the little chick had to struggle to stand up straight because of its wound. Then, as soon as it was standing, one of the other chicks would run over and bump it until it fell down. Now, that's very sad, but I didn't cry. Instead, I laughed until my sides ached.

My girlfriend stared at me. "Mike, you're not really *laughing* about this, are you?" she asked. I got defensive. Something inside me knew she was hitting close to home. "What do you mean, I'm not really laughing? What are you, some kind of psychiatrist or something?" I couldn't let her know she had touched on a sensitive subject, yet her message had gone straight to my heart. I knew God was trying to point out something to me.

Later on, in my room, I knelt and prayed. "God, what did she mean, 'You're not really laughing?' What was she getting at?" Then, the Lord reminded me of an incident that happened to me in grammar school.

I was a supersensitive kid in grammar school. Maybe it had something to do with my broken home life. I don't know. But I would cry at the drop of a hat. If something hurtful happened around me, I would weep. It didn't even have to involve me in any way.

One day in school, the class bully began picking on the class scapegoat right in front of me. As I watched the poor guy take a verbal beating, I could feel the tears forming in my eyes. I knew I was going to cry, but I didn't want to do it in front of my classmates. So, even though I didn't really find the situation humorous, I began to laugh, loud and hard, at that poor, defenseless kid.

I thought about the moment, running the scene over and over again through my mind. Then, God began to speak: *Mike, in that moment, you became your own defense. You became your own emotional shield, and you've never let it down. You've never let Me be your shield.*

You've never let Me be your protection. You've never let Me be your strong tower of defense.

The next day, I began to tell the same girl another sad story. As had happened the day before, I got to the tragic part and began to laugh. Again, she stared at me and said, "Mike, you're not *really laughing* about that, are you?"

"Wait a minute. Just wait a minute," I said. Then, I covered my face and became quiet. I wanted to allow my true feelings to surface. Soon, I was weeping. In that moment, I knew for the first time that God had become my emotional shield, my protector, and my strong tower of defense, and I was free to express my true self.

Perhaps in your own life, certain wounds have caused you to build walls and put up smoke screens. Perhaps the pain of separation or divorce has caused you to stop being genuine with others. Every time you're around someone, particularly of the opposite sex, you put on a mask. It's not the real you. It's a protective shield to keep you from ever being hurt again.

> **God has taken your wounds and frustrations from multiple rejections and borne them so you may know healing, wholeness, release, and freedom to love again in Him.**

God is saying to you today that you don't need those defenses any more. You don't need those masks. You've got a better one—the Lord Himself.

God desires for you to lay those defenses aside and trust completely in Him. He is calling you to take those hurts and release them to Him. God wants you to lay the wounds of that divorce, the anger of loss in widowhood, or the frustration and pain of multiple rejections that you may have experienced in the single life upon Him.

He has borne them for you so you may know healing, wholeness, release, and freedom to love again in Him.

Take hurt & baggy turn over to god.

Transitional Thought

Who Do You Think You Are?

When he was a little boy, my son Toby thought he was a great basketball player. He reached that conclusion one afternoon after playing a round of hoops with his friends.

Six-year-olds, you understand, know absolutely nothing about basketball technique. If the ball gets in the hoop, it's a miracle. But one day, Toby and his friends were playing around the hoop in their school yard, each of them winging the ball upwards in every unofficial form possible—double underhand, through-the-legs scoop shot; overhead, sling-forward-and-pray shot, and so on—trying to make it past the net, over the rim, and into the goal. One by one, each of Toby's friends tried to get the ball in but failed. Then, Toby's turn came. He hurled the ball upward with unusual effort, giving his throw just the added jolt it needed to send the ball over the rim, through the net, and down.

I can still remember his face as he jumped into the van beside me that afternoon. He was absolutely triumphant! "I made a basket, Dad! I made a basket!"

I smiled. "That's great, Toby! Really good. I'm so proud of you."

"Yeah," he said, a wide grin sliding across his face. For a moment, he was still. Then, looking over at me, he said, "Dad, do we have a basketball at home?"

"Yeah, I think we have one somewhere. I think there's an old one in the garage I can pump up for you."

"That would be good," he told me. "I think I'm really good at basketball."

A few weeks later, Toby and his friends went fishing. Knowing little to nothing about the subject, I tied a rubber beetle onto the end of his hook with the help of a friend and sent him off.

At the pond, Toby and his friends each dropped their hooks into the water. Most of them had live bait or at least some kind of food to attract the fish. Toby just had rubber. Slowly, one by one, each of Toby's friends began to get nibbles, but his own line remained deathly still.

At the end of the day, I went to pick him up. He dragged himself into the seat beside me, his face drooping with dejection. "How was fishing?" I asked, trying to boost his morale with a little bit of enthusiasm.

"I didn't catch anything," he said, a telltale tone of defeat in his voice.

"Well," I said, trying to uncover all the details of the situation, "did any of the other kids catch anything?" Perhaps if they hadn't, I thought, we could balance his emotions out a little bit with some calm, cool reasoning.

"Yeah. This one kid caught two fish, another kid got one, and everyone else got nibbles. I didn't get anything."

"Oh...."

Toby was silent for a while. Then, he looked at me and said, "I don't think I want to fish anymore, Dad. I don't think I'm very good at fishing."

The Deception of What Appears to Be

We adults can look at these situations and know there's more to them than meets the eye. We know that if by chance Toby had thrown that ball with a slightly different curve, he might have missed his important basket. We also know that if he'd had live bait, the chances of getting "nibbles" or even a fish would have been greatly increased. But in his little child's mind, Toby took those two isolated incidents and decided he was a terrific basketball player and a terrible fisherman. Neither one of those conclusions was based on facts, yet both went into my little boy's brain as part of his self-concept. His image of himself was being formed by what he perceived to be his successes and failures.

Many of us have the same kind of conclusions stored in our own heads about ourselves, and often, just like Toby's view of basketball and fishing, they bear no true revelation of our abilities. Yet they have shaped us and often limited us in many ways, sometimes in direct opposition to the very purposes for which God created us.

God has an amazing way of coming into our lives and blowing away our self-image. Moses' life was a case in point. Here was a man who, at the beginning of his life, had a pretty high self-image. He'd been raised in the courts of Pharaoh, had the best education available in his day, and was used to handling power and having things done when he said they were to be done.

Then, one day, everything turned sour. In an effort to champion the cause of righteousness in Egypt and, by his own strength, bring some sort of fair treatment to the Israelites, Moses killed an Egyptian to protect one of his own and tried to settle a dispute among two Israelites. During the second encounter, he found that his brethren rejected his efforts to solve their problem with a "who died and made you boss?" attitude and discovered that word had gotten out about the murder he committed. Fearing for his life, Moses fled Egypt. When, based on some outward successes, Moses believed he was capable and his self-image was high, God showed him that the image was faulty. Moses was not all-powerful as he supposed.

What followed were forty years in the desert. Moses felt worthless, powerless. His high self-image was replaced by an extremely low one. Now, because of experiencing forty years of isolation and separation from the halls of power, he believed he was a zero.

In the midst of this period of low self-esteem, God came to Moses and told him that he had been chosen to lead the Israelites out of bondage. Speaking from his warped, negative self-perception, Moses said, "Who am I, God, to do this thing? Nobody would accept my word. What authority do I have? I'm not the right person for the job."

Again, Moses' self-perception was out of whack with God's vision and purpose for his life. He had gone from being a superstar to being a nobody, and neither was true. "Who are *you*?" God implied. "Don't you understand? It doesn't *matter* who you are. I will be with you and I'll give you everything you need to say. And if I'm with you, who or what can stand against you?"

The Real You: Who God Says You Are

Each of us has a sense of who we are, scraped together from the patchwork of experiences in our lives and colored by our own perception of reality, the affirmation or rejection of others, and so on. But if we want to really latch on to God's purpose for our lives, we need to take that self-image with a grain of salt. Whatever our image is, positive or negative, it likely has little connection to the real truth and can even make us miss the very thing God has designed us to do.

If you're going to be a growing, changing, expanding person, walking in line with God's purposes for your life, you need to be willing to lay down the sense of who you think you are and *let God define you*. Remember, He's the One who chooses the weak to confound the strong, the foolish to overcome the wise, and the base and despised to bring down that which is noble. (See 1 Corinthians 2:27–29.) He's the One who chooses you.

Your singleness is no more a disqualifier for service than Toby's poor day at fishing was an indication of being a terrible fisherman. Don't let it determine your degree of usefulness to God. Instead, allow Him to speak His goals and purpose into your life and shape and use you according to *His purposes*. Remember, He's with you. Who or what—past, present, or future—can stand against you?

STUDY **(4)** GUIDE

Questions for Knowing and Growing

| 93 | 1. According to Mike, singleness is not a sign of rejection but a matter of what?

▶ 2. Do you agree or disagree with this statement? Why?

| 94 | 3. Why is he convinced his conclusions are true?

| 95 | 4. What, if anything, does your singleness signify?

▶ 5. Have you ever thought of your singleness as a sign that you were a "reject"? What has this done to your self-concept? How has it affected your relationships with others? List some ways you might overcome such obstacles.

5-96 6. God has provided a biblical program for dealing with the rejections and hurts of our lives. What is the Scripture passage Mike uses for his discussion of that program?

▶ 7. Read through that passage again and pay attention to those verses that God seems to impress on you. Record them here or underline them in your own Bible.

97 8. What is the exchange God makes for our rejection and hurt through the cross?

00-101 9. Because of this, what can you do with the pain of rejection in your life?

101 10. What else did Christ bear at the cross besides rejection and hurt?

103 11. How did Mike (and how can you) become free to express grief?

▶ 12. In this chapter, Mike talks about a common experience: laughing at an inappropriate moment to cover real feelings of hurt, rejection, or fear. How do you deal with these emotions? How do you think you might implement the passage of Scripture Mike quotes to more freely express your true inner emotions?

Doing the Word

1. In this chapter, Mike recalls his rejection from the Little League team and the freedom that came when, as an adult, he laid aside the limitations that rejection had caused and played softball with the men from his church. In doing so, he found that the power of God was there to enable him to get beyond his hurt and fear and live a fuller life.

Choose to do some activity that you have stayed away from because of past rejections, applying your trust in the Lord to the situation. Discover your reaction. What does God reveal to you through the new experience?

2. Pinpoint one area of hurt or rejection that you know is limiting your walk with God. Study what the Word of God has to say about the situation from which your hurt and rejection came and what course of action it suggests to remedy it. Take practical steps to follow the Word.

A GIFT FOR SERVICE

Your singleness is a gift from God for service.

L IKE NO OTHER TIME IN YOUR LIFE, YOUR SEASON AS a single person sets you free to serve God in a wholehearted and undistracted way. Unencumbered by many of the duties and responsibilities that go along with the married life, you are able to say "yes" to God in a dynamic way. You are free to throw yourself with abandon into the things of God—to know Him as you have never known Him before, to love Him in an intimate way, and to serve Him with all your heart, soul, mind, and strength—100 percent.

The apostle Paul was a single Christian who knew and appreciated this fact. He said in 1 Corinthians 7:32–35 (emphasis added),

> *But I want you to be free from concern. One who is unmarried is concerned about the things of the Lord, how he may please the Lord; but one who is married is concerned about the things of the world, how he may please his wife, and his interests are divided. And the woman who is unmarried, and the virgin, is concerned about the things of the Lord, that she may be holy both in body and spirit; but one who is married is concerned about the things of the world, how she may please her husband. **And this I say for your own benefit; not to put a restraint upon you, but to promote what is seemly, and to secure undistracted devotion to the Lord.***

Let's look at that last verse, where Paul shares with us the complete goal of his counsel to singles.

What is that goal? *"To promote what is seemly* [right, decent, expedient], *and to secure undistracted devotion to the Lord."* Paul was in no way saying that marriage is wrong. He was encouraging Christians to see the benefits of the single life and to spend it in total consecration and commitment to the Lord and His purposes. He urged singles to be devoted to the Lord and to give Him all of their attention, time, and talents.

> God urges singles to be devoted to the Lord and to give Him all of their attention, time, and talents.

As a single person, you have been given a unique opportunity to know God in the same special way Paul knew Him. He has given you a season in which you may know Him deeply, undistracted by any other concerns.

Just what did Paul mean by *"undistracted devotion"*? The Greek word for "undistracted" in this portion of text means "to be constantly attendant upon," or "to be sitting near." It's a servant's term, and it describes the kind of servant who is so focused on his master that just the slightest eye movement or gesture of need will send that servant into action. Let me show you what I mean.

A little while ago, I went to Dallas, Texas, to speak at a local church. As often happens, the pastor took me out to lunch after the service. We went to a Chinese restaurant.

Now, this restaurant was *really* Chinese. It had red chairs, red walls, and red tablecloths. A hand-painted Chinese calendar hung on the wall behind the cash register and Chinese lanterns dangled from the ceiling. It was even staffed with Chinese hosts, servers, and bussers.

Our server was an efficient woman, well versed in the English language. But our table attendant (the person who actually did all the serving) was a recent immigrant, and it showed. Still learning English, she was in that uncomfortable place of understanding a lot of what she heard but not wanting to respond. (She didn't want to make an awful mistake and be embarrassed by her own cumbersome handle on the new language.) So, she just kept quiet and went about her business.

We ordered, and our attendant came to fill our glasses with water. While we waited for our meal, the pastor and I passed the time chatting. My throat got a little dry, so I reached for my glass of water and took a sip.

Immediately, out of the corner of the room, our attendant came over and refilled my glass. I thought, *Well, that's nice,* so I nodded at her, and she nodded at me. Then, she walked away.

I was impressed. *Well, isn't that something?,* I thought. I didn't even have to say, "More water." I just drank a little bit, and she appeared immediately. What service!

The pastor and I talked a while longer, and the meal still hadn't arrived. I got thirsty again, so I reached over, grabbed my glass, and took another sip of water.

Immediately, the attendant ran over and filled my glass. I nodded to her once more. She nodded at me. I nodded again. She did the same. (This was getting ridiculous.) Finally, she walked away.

I shook my head in disbelief. In most restaurants, I practically had to start a fire in the ashtray to get anyone to come to my table. But here she was, running up to serve me at my slightest indication of need. I have to admit that I felt a little intimidated and found myself hesitating to take another drink for fear that she would feel obligated to come over again.

The meal finally came, and I looked around the table for some salt. Well, this incredibly attentive woman noticed the slight movement of my head and came running over to see what I needed.

I can still remember her staring into my face with this look that said, "What do you want?" I said, "Salt," and she ran off and got me some. Isn't that incredible?

What I want you to see is this: that woman was *constantly* attendant upon me. I didn't need to speak. I didn't even need to signal. Just a slight movement of my head was enough to tell her I needed something.

That's exactly the way God wants you to respond to Him, too. He doesn't want to have to yell to you across the room: "Hey you! I need something." He wants you to be so attentive to Him that just the slightest movement of His eye will be able to prompt you to action.

> *I will instruct thee and teach thee in the way which thou shalt go. I will guide thee with mine eye. Be ye not as the horse, or as the mule, which have no understanding: whose mouth must be held in with bit and bridle.* (Psalm 32:8–9 KJV)

God is calling single adults to be guided by the counsel of His eye. He does not want to have to lead you forcibly, as a horse or mule is led by bit and bridle.

Do you remember a time from childhood when your parents had guests over for dinner? You were all gathered around the table eating and someone passed you a plate of snacks. You reached out to grab a fistful—as usual—and, all of a sudden, you felt your mother glaring at you. She didn't have to say a word. You knew you were out of order. Quickly, you withdrew your hand, dropping most of what you had.

What happened? Your mother let you know, with just a look, that you were misbehaving. She guided you with the counsel of her eye.

God wants to be able to do the same thing with you as you walk with Him. He wants you to be so attentive to Him and know Him so well that just the slightest gesture on His part will tell you what He wants from you.

But what happens to many singles is that they get distracted. They're distracted by their desire for marriage. They're distracted by some career objective. They're distracted by this concern, that relationship, or those children, and it forces God to use extraordinary means to get their attention.

Some of these concerns and desires are good ones. There's nothing wrong with desiring a mate, caring for your children, or working well on the job. But when those things take on such astronomic proportions that they crowd out the voice of God in your life, it's time to make some changes.

> God is looking for single people who are fully attentive to Him, waiting upon Him, looking to Him, and yielded completely to His will.

If God has to knock you down every time He talks to you, doesn't that say something? Doesn't that tell you something is out of whack? Doesn't that tell you that something is wrong in your relationship with Him? What if every time I wanted to get my son's attention, I had to hit him on the head and yell, "Can you hear me?" That wouldn't indicate we had much of a relationship, would it?

But that's the way many singles force God to deal with them. They wait for Him to do something earth-shattering. They wait to hear an audible voice or witness a miracle. They wait to see His word to them skywritten before they respond to His call.

But God doesn't want it that way. He doesn't want to have to take drastic measures. He wants us to be counselled by His eye.

God is looking for single people who are fully attentive to Him, who are waiting upon Him, and who are looking to Him, completely yielded to His will. He's looking for those who are constantly attentive to Him, saying, "Here I am, Lord. Send me."

You've got to reach a point in your relationship with God where you are totally attentive to Him and yielded to His purposes. You've got to be so in tune with Him that you know what God wants you to do by His slightest gesture. And you must be ready to do it for Him, right then and there.

Understand me. I'm not talking about living your life in a super-spiritual, ethereal hover. I don't mean to suggest that you ask God about every minute aspect of your life. For instance, "God, should I brush my teeth this morning?" I'm talking about being committed—heart and soul—to the Lord in a way that can be seen in your attitude and service toward Him. You should know deep in your heart, without reservation, that your life is committed and yielded to the will of God. *Whatever* He wants, you're ready to do it.

That's what Paul was trying to accomplish in 1 Corinthians 7:35. He was trying to develop a people—in this case, single adults—who would give the Lord undistracted devotion.

Let's look at the way some of the other versions translate that verse. The King James Version says, "*That ye may **attend** upon the Lord **without** distraction*" (emphasis added). The *Revised Standard Version* says, "*To secure your **undivided** devotion to the Lord*" (emphasis added). The *Phillips Version* says, "*So that your service to God may be, as far as possible, **free** from worldly distractions.*"

No matter what version you look at, the message remains the same. God wants you to realize that your singleness is not a disease or a prison to be escaped at all costs. Neither is it an obstacle to be surmounted nor a wall to keep you out of the fullness of life. Your singleness is an opportunity to know Him intimately and to serve Him with your whole heart, soul, mind, and strength.

I believe God wants to develop three qualities in you that will enable you to give Him the absolute dedication He seeks.

116

The first is the ability to *give God all that you have*. The gospel of Mark contains an example of one who did just that.

> And He sat down opposite the treasury, and began observing how the multitude were putting money into the treasury; and many rich people were putting in large sums. And a poor widow came and put in two small copper coins, which amount to a cent. And calling His disciples to Him, He said to them, "Truly I say to you, this poor widow put in more than all the contributors to the treasury; for they all put in out of their surplus, but she, out of her poverty, put in all that she owned, all she had to live on." (Mark 12:41–44)

> Your singleness is an opportunity to know God intimately and serve Him with your whole heart, mind, soul, and strength.

Picture yourself among the disciples on that day. You've gone down to the temple with Jesus to watch people put offerings into the treasury. Unlike the quieter collections of today, it's a big show. Donors stroll in, one at a time, dressed in their finest attire. Some even have servants going before them, blowing trumpets to announce their arrival. There's no "don't let your left hand know what your right hand is doing" behavior going on here. The contributors want their audience to know just how much they're willing to give.

One by one they stroll up to the coffer, drag out huge sacks of money, and begin pouring their shiny gold offering into the box. The crowd "oohs" and "ahhs" as the coins pour out, glittering in the sunlight. Each offering is bigger than the one before.

Then, quietly and unobtrusively, a tiny widow appears on the scene. There is no fanfare for her. In fact, almost no one in the crowd notices her—no one but Jesus. He watches as she pulls two copper coins out of her pocket and drops them into the treasury.

Suddenly, Jesus begins to motion to His disciples. They gather around Him, and He asks, "Did you see that offering?" Immediately, they start talking about the large sums poured out by bejewelled rabbis in yards of rich clothing.

"No, I mean the woman...." The disciples have to think about it for a moment before they recall who she is. "Oh, yes...the widow...."

"That woman," Jesus said, "gave more than anyone else." They can't believe what they're hearing. "What do you mean, she gave more than everyone else? Didn't You see the guy with the bags of gold and the trumpeters?"

Jesus explained, *"They all put in out of their surplus, but she, out of her poverty, put in all she owned, all she had to live on"* (Mark 12:44).

That single woman, Jesus was saying, gave *all* that she had. She didn't hold back half for herself. She didn't excuse herself, saying, "Well, I'm a little low this week." She took everything she had—every last cent—and gave it to the kingdom of God.

In the same way, you need to be willing to give God all that you have. You need to be willing to pour out everything in worship, thanksgiving, and service to Him.

Now, understand me. I'm not talking about finances alone. I'm talking about giving the Lord everything you are and everything you have. I'm talking about surrendering your possessions, your abilities, your talents—even your desire for relationships, position, and authority—to Jesus Christ in total submission. I'm talking about saying, "Lord, here's everything I am—my abilities, my talents, and my skills. Here's everything I own—my car, my home, and my salary. Here's everything I long for—marriage, career, position, authority, and fame. I pour all of it out before You. It's no longer mine. It's Yours. Use it and dispose of it wholly according to Your will."

Sound radical? It *is*. Yet only when you are willing to give everything you are, everything you have, and everything you ever hope to be to the Lord can you truly be undistractedly devoted to Him. Only when you are willing to pour your whole self out as a sacrificial offering to God to use as He sees fit will you be able to serve Him without being distracted by other needs, drives, or desires. When you give it all to Him, you'll be able to focus your heart completely upon the Lord and serve Him and Him alone.

Unfortunately, a lot of singles have missed the boat on this issue. They've bought the world's message to them about single living: "You're single. Now's the time to do what you want to do and see what you want to see. You're free. You're free."

When you give everything to God, you'll be able to focus your heart completely upon the Lord and serve Him and Him alone.

But for the Christian single, that's not true at all. Your singleness is not your own. It belongs to God because *you* belong to God.

That means all the freedom you have, all the talents you have, all the abilities you have, and all the time and resources you have are not for spending on yourself. They're for spending on God and His purposes. Like no other time in your life, your time as a single person can be poured out fully and completely in service to Him.

What an incredible place you are in right now! What ability you have, as a single adult, to be used by God. You're unencumbered by the restraints of married life. You're free to serve the Lord—wherever and whenever He wants you to. Now *that's* exciting!

But certain liabilities inherent in the single lifestyle itself can present barriers that keep you from realizing this freedom to serve in everyday life. Because you are a single person, your life has an innate tendency to revolve solely around you. Who buys your clothes? For whom do you make dinner? Whom does your livelihood support? *You.*

Just by its nature, single living is a self-centered lifestyle and, as such, carries with it the tendency for the single person to become self-involved and depressed. It takes special effort, therefore, for the single person to look beyond himself or herself to others. But it is a necessary thing to do and, the Scriptures say, intrinsic to living a fulfilled life.

"For whoever wishes to save his life will lose it, but whoever loses his life for My sake and the gospel's will save it" (Mark 8:35).

Do you want to find life in your singleness? Do you want to know fulfillment? Then you've got to be willing to make the effort to look beyond yourself to others. You've got to be willing to give all you have to God. If you will do that, God promises fulfillment beyond your wildest dreams.

"Seek first His kingdom and His righteousness; and all these things will be added to you" (Matthew 6:33).

That's a promise from the Lord Himself. God says if we will seek Him first—before our clothing, before our jobs, and before our desire for marriage, career, position, or honor—He will meet the needs of our life and bless us beyond all that we dare think, ask, or imagine.

Give the Best That You Have

The second quality God wants to develop in you so you can give Him undistracted devotion is the ability to *give Him the best that you have.* An example of this trait can be seen in the gospel of Mark:

And while He was in Bethany at the home of Simon the leper, and reclining at the table, there came a woman with an alabaster vial of very costly perfume of pure nard; and she broke the vial and poured it over His head. But some were indignantly remarking to one another, "Why has this perfume been wasted? For this perfume might have been sold for over three hundred denarii, and the money given to the poor." And they were scolding her. But Jesus said, "Let her alone; why do you bother her? She has done a good deed to Me. For the poor you always have with you, and whenever you wish, you can do them good; but you do not always have Me. She has done what she could; she has anointed My body beforehand for the burial. And truly I say to you, wherever the gospel is preached in the whole world, that also which this woman has done shall be spoken of in memory of her." (Mark 14:3–9)

Jesus was so satisfied with what this woman did that He said she would be remembered forever for doing it. Wouldn't you like Jesus to be able to say that about you? Wouldn't you like to have your life contribute something that meaningful? But what did she do, exactly? Let's take a closer look, because I believe you'll find that it's especially significant for you as a single person.

Commentators who have studied this passage in depth say that for a woman of that time period to have such an expensive perfume was rare indeed. They deduce, therefore, that it was most likely her dowry. In Jesus' day, customs required a woman who wanted to get married to present a dowry to the family of her intended spouse. That was the rule. No dowry, no wedding.

But this was not just an anointing—though that, in itself, was spectacular. It was a prophetic action, foretelling the suffering of the Savior. It was the woman's act of abandonment before her Lord, in thanksgiving and love, of her opportunity for marriage. In pouring out that precious ointment upon Jesus, she was telling Him, "Lord, I love You. I love You more than anything else in my life, *including* my right to marriage." Jesus knew this and treasured it. He knew she had given Him *the best that she had.*

121

For many singles, the best they have is their right to marriage. For as long as they can remember, they've dreamt about having a special someone to share life with. And there's nothing wrong with that desire. God knew it wasn't good for man to be alone, so, in the beginning, He created a helpmeet for him. But sometimes the desire for marriage takes on such astronomic proportions that it rivals God for attention. It distracts singles from serving Him with their whole hearts.

When I was serving as an associate pastor of a local church in upstate New York, a young single woman once came to me for counsel. She was depressed and discouraged. She had become interested in a young, single man in the church who didn't even know she was alive. You know the story.

Well, her desire for him grew until she became dominated by her crush. She was gripped by the fantasy of her hoped-for relationship with this fellow. The problem got so severe that it even affected her ability to participate in worship on Sunday. Just one look at this guy would send her into the depths of depression.

> Sometimes the desire for marriage takes on such astronomic proportions that it rivals God for attention.

Becoming truly upset about what was happening to her, she came to me for advice. Well, I want to be honest with you—I didn't know what to tell her. After listening to her story, I shared some Scripture passages with her and challenged her to do a few small things. But I didn't feel able to meet her need very well.

A few days later, I was walking downtown and the woman I had counseled came jogging toward me. As I looked into her face, I could see something had changed. Instead of being crestfallen and depressed, she showed a particular radiance. Obviously, something dramatic had happened to her. I had to know what had occurred, so I said, "Hey, you took terrific. What happened to you?" Then she told me this story:

> Yesterday morning, I was taking my usual jog along that big lake just north of the church, and I passed a cemetery. Inside the cemetery stood this huge, rough-hewn cross. I didn't remember having seen it before. All I knew was that something inside of me felt drawn to it.
>
> On an impulse, I ran inside the cemetery gate and began jogging toward the cross. When I got to it, I felt that I should begin digging a hole, right there in front of it. So I did. I clawed away at the grass and began making a hole. Then, again feeling prompted, I took my desire for a relationship with that guy in my hands and proceeded to bury it in that hole at the foot of the cross. Then, having covered the hole with dirt and grass, I turned and ran away.
>
> Mike, ever since that moment I've been a different person. I've been free from that desire and the discouragement and frustration that went with it. I feel terrific.

And so did I, just looking at her. In a very graphic way, that woman had been able to bury—literally—her desire for that man at the foot of the cross and be freed to serve the Lord wholly and without distraction.

Perhaps you can relate to this story. You've got a big desire for a relationship, and it literally consumes you. Sometimes, especially when you're alone at home on a rainy day, the thoughts of it so devour you that you're left powerless. You feel worthless and empty, too. You've placed your whole heart on that desire for relationship, and, because it isn't there, you feel completely drained.

It's no wonder that, with such a desire gobbling you up inside, you find no joy in your Christian walk. It's no wonder that you find yourself self-centered, weepy, uncontrollably depressed, and negative. You've placed your life and your definition of worth on whether or not you have a special someone in your life, and it's defeating you, wholly and completely.

With your eyes so centered on that desire, there is no way you're going to be able to serve Christ or even get to know Him very well. You're distracted by that desire, and it's robbing you—day after day after day—of joy, fulfillment, power, victory, and purpose.

But you can do something to alleviate the problem. You can take that desire and do what that single woman did. Bury it at the foot of the cross—not literally, necessarily, but at least in your heart. You can let go of the desire that's controlling your life. You can let go of your self-destructive dream and give it to the Lord.

Please understand me. I am not saying you should take a pledge to stay single forever. Neither am I saying you shouldn't have a desire to be married. But you must keep marriage in the proper perspective—that is, under the lordship of Jesus Christ.

When the best dreams of your heart—children, career, home, or family—are poured out before the Lord and relinquished to His lordship, then you will be able to seek Him first and give Him your undivided attention.

Do What You Can Do

The third quality God wants to develop in you so that you may give Him undistracted devotion is the ability to *do what you can do.*

The woman who anointed Jesus' feet practiced this quality. She took the oil that she had and poured it out before the Lord.

I'm sure she thought that anointing Jesus with oil was an insignificant gesture on her part. I'm sure she wasn't aware of the spiritual implications of the act. So, compared to the disciples, who were leaving behind homes, families, and jobs to follow Christ, her task was fairly simple. Oh, she gave the best that she had. We know that, and she knew that. But compared to what others were doing, it didn't look like much.

She could have been discouraged as she poured out that ointment. She could have looked at what she was doing and thought, *Gee, this is such a little thing to do for One who means so much to me.* And she could have allowed that thought to keep her from doing it. But because she didn't—because she did what she could do—she ended up being used in prophetic ministry before the Lord. And Jesus said that wherever the Gospel was preached, she would be spoken of and remembered for what she had done.

As a single person, you may often wonder whether your life will touch another's with significance. This thought comes into your head as a by-product of single living as a whole. You come home every night to an empty apartment, perhaps miles away from relatives and close friends. And you wonder, *If I died tonight, would anybody notice? Would anybody care? Or would my body just lie here for days before anyone came to find me?*

I know singles who think that way. They're sure they're insignificant. They're sure they're needed so little by others that they could die tomorrow without being missed. Now, that may not be the case, but when you come home night after night to an empty apartment, you can begin to feel that way.

Closely related to that discouraging thought is the longing to make a difference in the world around you, to count for something in someone else's life, and to be remembered. The woman in this Bible passage was. Why? Because she was willing to do what she could do.

Many singles look at their lives and get caught up in the things they cannot do. "I can't sing like so-and-so. I can't preach like so-and-so. I can't build things like so-and-so," they say. But in thinking that way, they discourage themselves from taking *any* action whatsoever and keep themselves from experiencing the fulfillment that could be theirs by doing what they could do.

God is not interested in having you tackle some mammoth task beyond your ability. He's not interested in having you sing like Cathy, type like Elaine, or organize big events like Jim. He's interested only in having you do what you can do.

If you're a typist, God wants you to use that skill to serve Him. If you're a server in a restaurant, God wants you to serve as though you were waiting on Him. If you're a mechanic, He wants you to work as if it were His car you were servicing. If you're a businessman, God wants you to deal honestly in a Christian manner, doing everything as unto Him. If you're gifted in music, writing, art, or dance, don't bury it. Use it for the glory of God. Do what *you* can do.

> God is not interested in having you tackle some mammoth task beyond your ability. He's only interested in having you do what you can do.

"But Mike, all I can do is set up chairs on Sundays. All I can do is usher. All I can do is greet people at the door." Great! Go ahead and do it. It doesn't matter what you do, as long as you do what you can. That's all God is looking for.

In the gospel of Matthew, Jesus told a parable about three servants, each of whom was called to do what he could do:

For it is just like a man about to go on a journey, who called his own slaves, and entrusted his possessions to them. And to one he gave five talents, to another, two, and to another, one, each according to his ability, and he went on his journey. Immediately the one who had received the five talents went and traded with them, and gained five more talents. In the same manner the one who had received the two talents gained two more. But he who received the one talent went away and dug in the ground, and hid his master's money. Now after a long time the master of those slaves came and settled accounts with them. And the one who had received the five talents came up and brought five more talents, saying, "Master, you entrusted five talents to me; see, I have gained five more talents." His master said to him, "Well done, good and faithful slave; you were faithful with a few things, I will put you in charge of many things, enter into the joy of your master." The one also who had received the two talents came up and said, "Master, you entrusted to me two talents; see, I have gained two more talents." His master said to him, "Well done, good and faithful slave; you were faithful with a few things, I will put you in charge of many things, enter into the joy of your master." And the one also who had received the one talent came up and said, "Master, I knew you to be a hard man, reaping where you did not sow, and gathering where you scattered no seed. And I was afraid, and went away and hid your talent in the ground; see, you have what is yours." But his master answered and said to him, "You wicked, lazy slave, you knew that I reap where I did not sow, and gather where I scattered no seed. Then you ought to have put my money in the bank, and on my arrival I would have received my money back with interest. Therefore take away the talent from him, And give it to the one who has the ten talents." For to everyone who has shall more be given, and he shall have an abundance; but from the one who does not have, even what he does have shall be taken away.

(Matthew 25:14–29)

Here we have three men. Each has been entrusted with a certain number of talents—one with five, another with two, and a third with one, each according to his ability.

I want you to recognize something right from the start: each person had a purpose. There wasn't one person the master overlooked. He didn't do what you or I might have. He didn't look at the capacity of the five-talent man and entrust his whole fortune to him, leaving the other two men to tag along, helping him out. He looked at their abilities and gave them each a purpose in keeping with his potential. Then, he went away, trusting them to use their talents wisely.

When he returned, he found that both the five-talent man and the two-talent man had used what was given to them prudently and had managed to double it for the master. But the one-talent man, being fearful, had buried his talent in the ground, doing nothing with it until the master returned. The master was exceedingly pleased with the work of the first two. They had been good stewards of their talents. But he rebuked the third man, calling him wicked and lazy.

It's important to note that the reward had nothing to do with the amount produced. It had to do with the degree of faithfulness in the servant to do what he could do. The five-talent man used his talents and doubled them. So did the two-talent man. Both used what they had to the fullest. But the one-talent man looked at what he had and buried it instead of using it to its full advantage.

Let's take a closer look. The five-talent man was the type of person you knew in school who could do everything well—he was quarterback on the varsity football team, leading man in the school play, and the best academic performer in his class.

But the two-talent man and the one-talent man were more or less equals. The two-talent man had several fine abilities. He was skilled in a few areas. The one-talent man also had ability—he was especially gifted in one particular way. Yet the ways these two responded to the master differed drastically. One did what he could with what he had. The other buried it and was chided.

What made the one-talent man bury his talent? From looking at my life and this passage of Scripture, I've come up with several reasons. First of all, he compared his abilities to those of the other two men. *That five-talent guy has so much ability. He could do a lot more than I could ever do—without even trying. That two-talent man has twice as much ability as I do. He'll do better than I will for sure. The best I could do would be pitiful compared to them, so I might as well just quit right now.*

Second, we see the master call the one-talent man "wicked" and "lazy." Could it be that the one-talent man used comparison as an excuse for laziness? How many times have you done that—used "I can't do this" or "I can't do that" as an excuse for personal laziness? You really don't *want* to reach. You really don't *want* to stretch. You really don't *want* to try. You'd rather stay where you are than go through the struggle that growing and giving 100 percent entails. This passage indicates that an element of laziness quenched the one-talent man's motivation.

Third, the man may have chosen to bury his talent because he feared failure. *What if I try and I fail? What if I do something and it doesn't measure up? I might as well bury it. If I do that, at least I can't lose it. If I put it in the ground, at least it won't get taken.* He wasn't willing to risk.

Fourth, this man misunderstood the master. He thought he would be judged based on how much he accomplished rather than on what he did with what he had.

Many singles suffer with the same problems that this one-talent man had. First, they compare themselves, ability for ability, with others. "I can't sing like Joanie. I can't play guitar like Sam. I can't speak in front of people like Max. I can't do street witnessing like Jamie." And they disqualify themselves from service.

Sometimes they're also lazy, making excuses for not serving God. "I'm not married yet. I'm too young. I'm too old. I'm a new

Christian. I've been wounded by divorce. I'm a single parent—I've got children to attend to." While some of these may be true and valid and have their roots in real areas of responsibility, there's a line over which you cross that becomes a wall erected to keep yourself from serving God: you've got a "good" excuse.

Many singles also become plagued by fear of failure. They have seen important relationships collapse before their eyes, despite all their attempts to restore them. Others have tried and failed at work. It's left them bruised and empty inside, fearful of trying—and failing—all over again. So, they adopt a "no-risk" mentality. "If I don't try, at least I'll never be disappointed. If I don't try, at least I won't fail." But thinking like that only keeps them from growing in Christ and doing what God calls them to do.

Listen to me. God is not concerned about what Jamie or Bobby can do that's "better" than what you can do. He's concerned only with having *you* do what *you can do.* If that's setting up chairs on Sunday, fine. If it's typing letters for the pastor, great. If it's balancing the accounts in a bank or other business, terrific. If it's singing, playing an instrument, or speaking, wonderful. *Whatever* you can do, God wants you to do that.

> God expects you to use the talents, abilities, and skills you *do* have for His glory.

He doesn't have any expectations of you that exceed the abilities you have. He knows what you can accomplish—as well as what you can't. He knows what abilities He's given to you, and He doesn't expect more from you than them.

But He does expect you to do what you can do. He does expect you to use the talents, abilities, and skills you *do* have—be they natural or instilled by the power of God—for His glory.

God doesn't look at the magnitude of the gift. He looks at the giver's ability to give. He doesn't look at the size of an offering but at the amount left in a person's pocket. He doesn't look at how much ministry a person does, only how much is held back. God is not concerned with how much you do, but that you do what you can with what you have.

So, there are three qualities that will enable you to give God undistracted devotion.

One: *Give all that you have.* Surrender every desire, every thought, every ability, and every personality trait to the lordship of Jesus Christ—and allow Him to use them as He sees fit.

Two: *Give the best that you have.* Be willing to surrender the supreme desire—be it for marriage, a new career, or a lifestyle—to Him to dispose of or reclaim wholly, according to His will. Make Him your supreme desire.

Three: *Do what you can do.* Take the talents, abilities, and skills God has bestowed upon you and use them for His glory.

If you will, by the grace and transforming power of God, be faithful to do these things, you'll find yourself undistractedly devoted to Him and reap the benefits besides: a whole, complete, satisfying, purpose-filled life in Christ.

Transitional Thought

The Professional Hugger

It's amazing how many singles think they have nothing to offer God in the way of talents and abilities. Not too long ago, I was down South visiting a Christian day care program for poor families.

The program was a real inspiration to me. It was started by a group of single women who had a burden to reach the inner city for Christ. These women got together and bought a home near a housing project in their city and began offering a free day care service to families. The only requirement was that the adults in each participating family become involved in a weekly Bible study.

It wasn't long before oodles of little children with runny noses and dirty faces were crowding into the house, and families were getting saved. I can still remember how good it felt the day I entered that house and saw the kids milling around me, giving me hugs. Their faces were sunny and they looked so hungry for love.

On Sunday, as I prepared to leave, the director caught me by the arm. "Mike," she said, "I know you meet a lot of people in your travels and I was thinking maybe you could help us. We need somebody to come and work with us. It might be good if he had his own income or perhaps was retired, something like that."

"What exactly do you want this person to do?" I asked.

"Well, what we'd like this person to do," she explained, "is just come and sit down in the living room and hug the kids."

I couldn't believe what she was saying. It seemed so simple, so easy. "Wait a minute. Are you telling me you want something like a professional hugger?"

She nodded. "The staff here is involved in all different projects and these kids have a special need for affection and love. They've been denied it so much in their lives. But we just don't have the time to give them all the physical contact and support they need. We thought if we could have somebody who was specially dedicated just to loving the kids, it would help so much."

Someone Out There Needs You

As she spoke, I thought about all the places I travelled to and the people I spoke to whose lives were wrapped around themselves: "Who cares about me? Who wants me?" And here were all these kids who only needed people who would take time out of their lives to give them simple hugs, words of praise—just give them love. It didn't take a special person with particular talent or ability to do that job. Anybody with a big heart could do it.

Today, right where you are, there are people who need you. You don't need to be especially bright or beautiful. You don't need years and years of experience. You just need a heart willing to do what you can to express the love of God to a needy world and a hurting church. God can use you today. He can use you to give a smile to a weary bank clerk, to put your arm around a discouraged coworker, to set up chairs for your church meeting, to help your son with his math homework, or to get groceries for the shut-in down the street. There are myriad opportunities for service, and they don't require a Bible degree or college diploma—only a heart to serve and hands that are willing to do what they can do. Will you do what you can today?

STUDY **5** GUIDE

Questions for Knowing and Growing

| 111 | 1. What is your singleness a gift for?

.

| 111 | 2. Why can you serve God so well as a single?

| 111-112 | ▶ 3. What did the apostle Paul have to say about singleness? Read the passage of Scripture, then express Paul's ideas in your own words.

| 112 | 4. What is the goal of singleness, according to Paul?

| 112 | 5. What does it mean to be "undistractedly devoted" to God?

4   6. Mike tells the story of a young, Chinese restaurant table attendant who gave him outstanding service. What did she do that Mike says God wants singles to do in their relationship to Him?

4   7. What passage of Scripture does Mike quote to help you understand this principle?

▶ 8. What are some things that keep singles from giving God the undistracted devotion He seeks? Can you think of some more examples from your own life?

▶ 9. What, in your opinion, makes singles become so distracted by these things? What might be done to enhance a single person's ability to give God the undistracted devotion He seeks?

6   10. What place must you reach in your relationship with God in order to give Him the kind of devotion He seeks?

117-124 11. What are the three qualities (pages 117, 120, and 124) that need to be in a single's life in order for him or her to give God the undistracted devotion He seeks?

117 12. What illustration from Scripture does Mike use to teach about the need for singles to give "all that they have"?

13. Why did the widow give more than the others?

118-119 14. What, similarly, do singles need to be willing to give?

119 15. What message have singles "bought" from the world that has short-circuited their ability to tap into this life of wholehearted service?

120 16. Are singles really free? What, in contrast, does Mike have to say on the subject?

120 17. What does this mean for the single Christian?

▶ 18. What liabilities can present barriers to realizing this freedom to serve?

20 | 19. How can you escape these barriers and find fulfillment in your singleness?

20-121 | 20. What biblical illustration does Mike use to teach singles to give the best that they have and do what they can do? Read the passage again and record it here in your own words.

▶ 21. How does this passage illustrate these two principles?

22 | ▶ 22. Mike mentions one thing that singles consider "the best that they have" that can short-circuit a wholehearted desire to love and serve the Lord. What is it? How, by the illustration Mike gives on page 123, can we deal with such hindrances?

▶ 23. What other things can you see in a single person's life that, left unsurrendered to God, could keep him or her from living completely, wholeheartedly for Him? What kind of remedies would you suggest for each of these things?

▶ 24. What is "the best" that you have in your life? Is it a dream of marriage? A desire for family, career, home, stability, or financial success? Have you offered that "best" to God with no strings attached? If so, share the experience in which that happened. If not, discuss the times God may have put His finger on that "best" and requested it, some of the reasons you've had a hard time letting go of it, and some course of action you might take to help you let go of it today.

▶ 25. Have you ever had the feeling that you could die tomorrow and nobody would know? What has contributed to that attitude?

▶ 26. What could you do that would help diffuse this feeling of worthlessness in yourself or others?

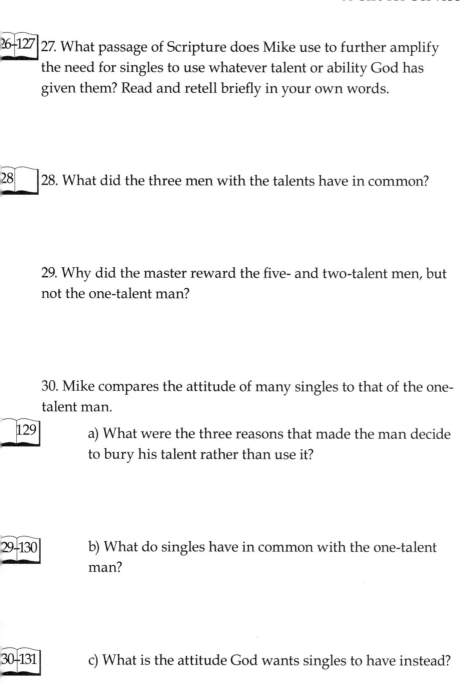

26-127 27. What passage of Scripture does Mike use to further amplify the need for singles to use whatever talent or ability God has given them? Read and retell briefly in your own words.

28 28. What did the three men with the talents have in common?

29. Why did the master reward the five- and two-talent men, but not the one-talent man?

30. Mike compares the attitude of many singles to that of the one-talent man.

129 a) What were the three reasons that made the man decide to bury his talent rather than use it?

29-130 b) What do singles have in common with the one-talent man?

30-131 c) What is the attitude God wants singles to have instead?

131 31. What will happen to those who cultivate the three qualities discussed in this chapter?

▶ 32. Study the three qualities singles should have in order to give God undistracted devotion. Are these qualities found in your own life? How could you cultivate such qualities and find expression for them in your own life?

▶ 33. Examine the talents God has given you. Which one(s), if any, have you buried, and why? How can you find ways to express them?

Doing the Word

Have the singles in your church make a list of the various talents and abilities God has given them. Then, list the needs of your church. Devise a plan for pooling your singles' resources to meet the needs and present it before your pastor for implementation.

Discover Your Purpose

*Your singleness provides you with a special opportunity
to discover your purpose in Christ.*

THAT'S RIGHT. YOUR SINGLENESS NEED NOT BE MERELY
an interim period in which you wait for life to begin. It can and
should be a time to serve the Lord fully in the purpose He has created just for you.

God has a special plan for your life that doesn't have to wait for
marriage in order to be fulfilled. It's a purpose He's created just for
you and for which He has equipped you and you alone.

How do you know what God's specific purpose is for you? I
believe it can be found, first of all, in the fabric of your own being—
the blueprint God created for you while you were yet in your mother's womb. Jeremiah 1:5 says, *"Before I formed you in the womb I knew
you, and before you were born I consecrated you; I have appointed you a
prophet to the nations."*

Isn't that a staggering thought? Before Jeremiah was even born,
God knew him and had a plan for his life. Just as surely, God has
known you and has a plan for you.

> *For You formed my inward parts; You wove me in my moth-
> er's womb. I will give thanks to You, for I am fearfully and
> wonderfully made; wonderful are Your works, and my soul
> knows it very well. My frame was not hidden from You, when*

I was made in secret, and skillfully wrought in the depths of the earth; Your eyes have seen my unformed substance; and in Your book were all written the days that were ordained for me, when as yet there was not one of them. (Psalm 139:13–16)

Here, again, we realize that God has been involved with our lives since before we were born. Before our mothers even sensed our presence, God knew us. More than that, He was actively involved in our formation—in the features and the coloring we would have, the talents and skills we would possess, and the temperament through which He would display His glory. He planned it all so that one day we would glorify Him in a particular way.

That means *nothing* inside of us is an accident. Our skills, our talents, our looks, and our abilities—everything we are—were put in us for a purpose: that we may fulfill *His* purpose for our lives.

> We can look at who we are humanly and get a fairly good indication of the person God has called each of us to be.

That means we can look at who we are humanly and get a fairly good indication of the person God has called each of us to be. If we're talented in art, God wants to use us in that way. If math is our strong suit, God wants to use that ability to glorify Himself. If we enjoy serving others as a host, caterer, custodian, homemaker, child care worker, or flight attendant, that is no accident, either. God has put a heart in us for that kind of work, and He wants to glorify Himself through us. If you're a mechanic, a body worker, an engineer, a bus driver, a conductor, a warehouse worker, or a salesperson, God wants to use you for His glory. There's no limit to what He can do. All you need to do is be aware of the talents He's given you and use them.

You can look, too, at your family background, your home life, your education, your training, your religious affiliation, and your social interests to find still more clues. Oh, your background may be filled with all sorts of non-God-glorifying events. Your parents may have been divorced or you may have been an orphan. You may have had a secular upbringing during which God was never mentioned. Maybe you had a bad period of rebellion—taking drugs, drinking, participating in immoral activities, even disdaining those who believed in God and chiding them to their faces. That certainly wasn't God's will for your life. But today, as a Christian, you can take a new look at the fabric of your life and allow God to weave it into the marvelous plan He has prepared especially for you.

> *And we know that God causes all things to work together for good to those who love God, to those who are called according to His purpose.* (Romans 8:28)

Today, as a Christian single, you love God and have been called according to His purpose. Therefore, God wants to use everything you are, everything you can do, and everything you've ever been through to bring Him glory and honor and produce fruits of righteousness in the earth.

You can look at your environment—and your response to it—and see a reflection of what God has called you to be in His kingdom. What did you enjoy doing in school? What things inspired you? What kind of experiences made you want to excel? What was your home life like? What kind of religious upbringing did you have? What extracurricular activities did you enjoy? All these things can provide clues to the purpose God has for your life.

"But, Mike, what if I look at myself and don't see anything particularly outstanding? What if I see a minus thirty-five?"

Well, I know just how you feel, believe me. All I need to do is take one look at my own life to know that nothing in it recommended me for service. A shy, gawky, overly sensitive kid, I was an average student. I got mostly Cs. As far as home life goes, mine wasn't exactly the best. I grew up in a single-parent household. My church background was minimal, and I had no real relationship with God—just an outer coating of religious training.

When I looked at my life, I didn't see much God could use. But God spoke to me, as He did to Jeremiah, and told me—a shy, nervous kid—that I, of all people, was going to be "a prophet to the nations." More than that, He took me, a married person, and gave me a ministry to singles. Isn't that unbelievable? Yes, it really is. Yet God has moved in my life, equipped me for the ministry He's called me to, and caused the impossible to happen.

How did it get accomplished? By His grace. You can look at your life and not see much to recommend you for service. But that doesn't matter in the kingdom of God. What God calls you to do, He equips you for—by natural abilities, yes, but also (and most importantly) by His grace.

It doesn't matter if you have only a limited education, lack skill in sports, have physical disabilities, are shy or nervous, are old or young, or lack any other thing you think is necessary for service. God can and will use you. He will enable you *by His grace.*

I once taught a class at a Bible school, and I met a young woman who had cerebral palsy. Her body was crippled, but her attitude about life certainly wasn't. She wrote a story about living with her handicap. I'd like to share it with you.

What's It Like?

What's it like being handicapped? Well, it's hard for the handicapped to accept what they have. Other people make fun of them. Some people who have handicaps give up. They think they can't do things. They can if they try.

I'm handicapped. I have cerebral palsy. I wanted to give up, but I didn't. I went on. Also, I'm a Christian, and that means I belong to Jesus forever and ever. My handicaps belong to Him now.

I'd like to tell you a story that happened to me. My doctor told me that I wouldn't be able to play the piano because I didn't have enough strength in my fingers. I took piano lessons for four years. I didn't give up. Now I play hymns and Christian music all the time. And when I play them, they are prayers to Jesus.

People think I can't do things because of my handicaps. But I go roller skating, drive a car, sing, and many other things. These are gifts that God has given to me.

Look at Joni Eareckson. She's in a wheelchair, and she didn't give up. She went on like me. Even though she's paralyzed from the neck down, she can drive a van. Joni loves the Lord and travels all over the world and preaches.

Sometimes people feel sorry for us. We don't need that at all. God has a plan for me, and I must be patient and ready to do His will. *"I can do all things through Him who strengthens me"* (Philippians 4:13).

This young woman could have chosen to be discouraged and defeated in life. Instead, she saw her potential in Christ and was able to believe Him for great things. Humanly speaking, many limitations were placed on this girl's life. But, by God's grace, she remained optimistic and believed He would use her for great exploits in His kingdom.

The more reasons you can list why God shouldn't use you, the more He sees you as a prime candidate for service. Second Corinthians 4:7 says, *"But we have this treasure in earthen vessels, that the surpassing greatness of the power may be of God and not from ourselves."*

Have you ever gone into a greenhouse and seen a beautiful plant inside a rather homely pot—the plant is gorgeous, but the pot you could do without? That's the way God likes to be inside us. He likes to be the beautiful plant inside your ordinary clay pot. When He is, people get caught up with Him rather than you, and that's His objective. He wants to get the glory.

The more you look at yourself and see what disqualifies you for service, the more God wants to use you. When He uses you, everyone will know that it's God.

> *For consider your calling, brethren, that there were not many wise according to the flesh, not many mighty, not many noble; but God has chosen the foolish things of the world to shame the wise, and God has chosen the weak things of the world to shame the things which are strong, and the base things of the world and the despised, God has chosen, the things that are not, that He might nullify the things that are, that no man should boast before God.* (1 Corinthians 1:26–29)

Do you look at your life and see weakness? Do you feel despised, rejected, and worthless? Do you feel too old, too young, or too unable? Great! God wants to use you. In fact, you're the very person He's looking for. In you, He can really shine. The apostle Paul grasped this idea readily and rejoiced,

> *Most gladly, therefore, I will rather boast about my weaknesses, that the power of Christ may dwell in me. Therefore I am well content with weaknesses, with insults, with distresses, with persecutions, with difficulties, for Christ's sake; for when I am weak, then I am strong.* (2 Corinthians 12:9–10)

If you look at your life—that marriage that ended in divorce, that body depleted with age, that much-scarred ego wounded by rejection—and think God can't use you, I want you to know you're wrong. He not only can but He wants to, even more than you want to be used by Him. You were created for a purpose, and despite all the things you see that make you sure you can't be used by God, He will see that purpose fulfilled.

God will take any painful experience of singleness and use it for His glory. But you must take who you are and what you've experienced—both the bad and the good—and offer it to Him. Today, if you will yield every talent, every ability, every fault, every weakness, and every wound to the Lord, He will begin to use those things to bear everlasting fruit in His kingdom.

The Importance of Vision

God does not want us wandering aimlessly, yielding ourselves to every cause that comes along. He wants us channeled into specific realms of service. To do that, we need a sense of *personal vision*. Personal vision gives us a long-range objective to shoot for that keeps us "in line" in the here and now. Personal vision gives us a view of where and how God wants us to serve Him ultimately that affects the way we live today.

A sense of personal vision gives scope and dimension to our lives—parameters within which we operate today to help fulfill God's ultimate will for our lives. Without this sense of vision, a person will have a tendency to drift, and his resistance to temptation will be low.

Proverbs 29:18 says, *"Where there is no vision, the people are unrestrained."* People without vision live careless lives. Undirected by an ultimate objective, they have a tendency to wander off course, to waste time, and to lose conviction and motivation. They live day-to-day without any sense of the future, and it causes them to refrain from disciplines that could prepare them for it.

Most of us have experienced "the blues" that come in early spring when we realize we've gotten just a bit too chubby to climb into our summer clothing. All winter long, we sat in front of the television set, shoveling food into our mouths and gaining weight.

While the snow flakes fell, we hardly gave a thought to summer—at least not one that caused us to change the way we were taking care of ourselves during the cold winter months. Then, spring came, along with thoughts of the beach and swimming. Immediately, we saw ourselves sunning amid a wash of humanity. *No way am I putting a body like this on the beach*, we thought. And we began a mad rush of diet and exercise meant to get us slim and trim for summer.

> Personal vision gives us a view of where and how God wants us to serve Him ultimately that affects the way we live today.

All winter long, we lived careless lives without vision, and it caused us to become physically lazy and indulgent. Then, with the first twinge of spring, we got a vision of summer, and it inspired us to exercise discipline in diet and exercise so we might be ready to face the summer when it came.

A personal vision does the same thing for us spiritually. It gives us a vision of who God has called us to be and influences the way we live today. How can you receive a personal vision for your life? There are a number of ways.

The first way is through the Word of God itself. You will be reading the Word when, suddenly, a verse seems to come alive for you personally. God is speaking especially to you in that moment, and He gives you a vision for your life.

A second way vision is revealed is through Christian books. For example, you could be reading a biography of a great man or woman of God and begin to identify with that person's calling, struggles, beliefs, and life. In that instance, God might be tugging on your heart, directing you to—or confirming—a path He has chosen for your life.

A third way vision is revealed is through the confirming word of another person.

I remember a time during Bible school when the vice president of the school did that for me. A group of my classmates and I were gathered at his home for fellowship and discussion when, all at once, he turned to me and, with a perfect Welsh accent, said, "Mike, what do you want to do with your life?"

Now, Brother David Edwards was an astute man, so discerning, I thought, that he knew everything that went through my head. I was sure that even my most innocent statement could reveal more of me to him than I wanted him to know. That made me a little nervous whenever I spoke to him.

So, when he asked me this question, I wanted my answer to be good. I wanted him to be impressed. I shifted in my seat just slightly, then replied, "I want to do whatever God wants me to do, Brother Edwards. If God wants me to pump gas, I'll pump gas. If He wants me to sell insurance, I'll sell insurance. I'll do *anything* He wants me to do."

That's a spiritual answer, isn't it? It sounds good, doesn't it? But to Brother Edwards, it just didn't ring true. He leaned forward in his seat, drawing his face closer to mine. "Mike, what do *you* really want to do?" I thought again. I wanted to be honest, now—as honest as I possibly could be. Then, in a moment of boldness, I said, "I want to be the best preacher I can be."

Brother Edwards, who later became the president of that Bible school, was and is one of the most eloquent speakers I had ever heard. When he spoke in class or in chapel, his words carried with them the power and authority of God. So, saying I wanted to be the best preacher was a gutsy thing to do. I felt sure he would reprimand me or at least chide me for being so presumptuous.

But he didn't. Instead, he looked at me and said, "Well, why don't you go ahead and do it, then?" His words sunk deep into my spirit. *Yeah*, I thought, *why don't I?* And in that moment, with those few words, Brother Edwards released me to follow God's will for my life.

Setting Realistic Goals

Nothing is wrong with pumping gas, selling insurance, or any other thing God may want you to do. It's just not what the Lord was calling me to do. It wasn't what He had equipped me for.

Inside of you is something that you, personally, have been equipped by God to do. Perhaps you've been called to be a teacher, an administrator, a business executive, a secretary, a construction worker, a bookstore owner, a chef, or a mechanic. God has placed *that* purpose on your heart, and you want to fulfill it.

Well, chances are you're not that person now. That's just a vision God has given you. How do you go about progressing toward that vision? *By setting goals that you can accomplish now.*

What are goals? Goals are measurable purposes that enable us to walk, step by step, toward the vision God has for our lives. Let me give you some examples.

To be a great mountain climber is a vision; to climb Pike's Peak in January is a goal.

To reach a neighbor for Christ is a vision; to invite my neighbors to a Bible study in my home on December 10 is a goal.

Goals give us concrete ways to develop into the people God has called us to be and embrace the purpose He has set aside especially for us. They also give us a tangible way of measuring how far along we've come in that vision.

When God told me I was going to be "a prophet to the nations," I was nowhere near fulfillment of that calling. Inside, I still had a lot of growing to do.

But I earnestly desired to pursue God's call on my life and to "go ahead and do it," as Brother Edwards had said. So, I began doing what I could do. I called up the pastors of several local churches and asked if I could speak to their congregations. They refused. I was still so young and untried. What could I do?

Well, the school I attended had something called an "outstation" program. The purpose of the program was to give students practical experience in ministry in addition to their study time, while also helping local ministers with the work they needed to do.

One of the outstations served the downtown mission. There, street people could get a hot meal if they were willing to listen to someone preach for half an hour. "Would they let me preach?" I asked the person in charge of the outstation. "Sure," he told me, and that's how I began my preaching ministry—talking to a group of destitute men at an inner-city mission.

That doesn't sound much like a "prophet to the nations," does it? And I wasn't. Not yet. But I was growing, step-by-step, into that vision by accomplishing goals that were presently within my reach.

The same thing will be true for you. God may call you to be president of IBM, and that's great. But it isn't going to happen right away. You're going to be groomed for it first. Setting and achieving goals that you're able to accomplish now is the way that happens.

Goals are also *faith achievements* in which we reach out in faith and lay hold of the future. Right now, as founder and director of a nationwide single adult ministry, I'm reaching out and laying hold of the year ahead. I'm planning all our activities for next year in faith.

For you, it may not be as far-reaching. Perhaps it will only be a few months down the line, or less. But you *should* be reaching into the future and taking it by faith.

Get out there and volunteer to help the handicapped if you're called to the health care field. If education is your sphere, assist a local teacher in grading papers or tutoring students. Get out and help the local Right-to-Life group if law or social action is your calling. Assist a Christian counselor in her work if that's the area where God wants you to be.

There are thousands of ways to begin—thousands of places aching for dedicated people with a sense of vision and commitment to work with them. Go to your pastor if you need help finding a place to serve. Perhaps even advertise your availability in your church bulletin. Chances are, a member of your church is involved or burdened with the same calling or knows someone who is. Take the first step. Get involved.

And, above all, don't let fear or worry stop you. I know a lot of singles who won't set goals for themselves because they're afraid of failure. But it's impossible to fail totally if you dare to try. *Success involves risk.* And, in the Christian life, it's not taking risks by yourself but with God at your side. As Paul said, *"If God is for us, who is against us?"* (Romans 8:31).

> Don't let worry or fear of failure stop you. In the Christian life, you don't take risks alone, but with God by your side.

Not too long ago, I spoke at the Christ for the Nations Institute in Dallas, Texas. I stayed for a week, speaking each morning in their chapel service. After each session, the students would line up to talk to me at the speaker's platform, which stood a few steps up from the floor.

One day as we were chatting, I looked out into the auditorium and saw a little man in a wheelchair rolling toward the platform. He was a small, frail man; his legs just managed to reach out over the edge of his seat.

I watched as this man got a few of the students to help him up to the platform, where he got in line with the others. Finally, his turn came to speak to me. I bowed down to say hello, and he grabbed my hand. His eyes met mine, and without another word he began to speak.

> Far better it is to dare mighty things, win glorious triumphs, even though checkered by failure, than to take rank with those poor spirits who neither enjoy much nor suffer much because they live in the gray twilight that knows not victory nor defeat.

The words were Franklin Delano Roosevelt's, but it was obvious they held special meaning to this handicapped gentleman. "Mike," he said, still looking at me, "I *know* God is going to do something with my life." The man spoke with conviction. I knew that, despite all his physical disabilities, this man had a sense of personal vision. He was a person of destiny.

You, too, are a person of destiny. Since before you were born, God has had a plan for your life. That plan cannot be thwarted by any disability you have—physical, relational, or otherwise. No matter what you've been through, God can still use you. No matter how wounded you are, how powerless you feel, or how untalented and unskilled you perceive yourself to be, God has a plan for your life, and He is big enough to see that plan fulfilled in you today.

The only thing that can keep you from being what God wants you to be is an act of your will. You can choose to let the limitations you see keep you from experiencing fullness in Jesus Christ. You can allow the rejections and hurts of the past to bind you to a lonely, purposeless life. You can allow fear to hem you in on all sides and freeze you up so you never go anywhere in God.

Or, you can take all that you are—both in weakness and in strength—pour it out before the Lord, and experience healing, power, fulfillment, and usefulness in the kingdom of God.

God wants you to be fulfilled, and He wants you to have purpose and meaning. He wants you to be healed and freed of the hurt, rejection, and fears that have bound you. And He's provided a way through Jesus Christ, His Son.

If you will begin to trust Jesus today, lay all your burdens upon Him, and, in faith, begin to walk in the purpose He has laid upon your heart, you will begin to know joy, meaning, purpose, and wholeness. You'll discover that true fulfillment is not in any human relationship, no matter how deep, but in an ever-deepening relationship with Jesus Christ.

You possess within you the talent and ability to be used greatly in the kingdom of God. You possess the gifts and the skills needed to do what He has called you to do. And, most importantly, you possess His Holy Spirit—the Enabler and Empowerer—who will protect, guide, strengthen, and embolden you to do what God has called you to do. Trust in Him today, and begin living the life God has destined especially for you. *"Faithful is He who calls you, and He also will bring it to pass"* (1 Thessalonians 5:24).

Transitional Thought

The Little Boy and the Valentines

Bobby's mother was apprehensive as her little boy described the project their teacher had launched for Valentine's Day. "We're each going to make little mailboxes," he told her excitedly, "And then we're going to put cards for everybody in them. I want to make a card for everybody in the class!"

Bobby wasn't exactly the kind of child all the other kids flocked to, his mother realized. He was more of an outsider, and she was afraid he was in for great disappointment come February 14. What would happen, she wondered, when he gave a valentine card to every child in the class and his own box remained empty?

Not wanting to discourage him from his kindhearted idea, though, she helped him make his box and cards, one chosen carefully for each child in the class. The next morning, she kissed his forehead and sent him off to school.

The whole day, Bobby's mom thought about what might be happening to her son. *He's going to be so upset when he comes home,* she thought to herself.

Finally, 2:30 p.m. rolled around. The bus rumbled to a stop at the corner and Bobby came walking into the house. "How was your day?" Bobby's mom asked with gentle concern.

"Not one, mom. Not one," Bobby said. She tried to manage a faint smile. "Not one? What do you mean, Bobby?" she asked, imagining the worst.

Suddenly, he broke out into a wide grin. "We didn't miss one! We had a card for everybody!"

Half Empty or Half Full?

So many single people I meet look at the world through Bobby's mother's eyes. They're so concerned about others meeting their needs and showing them that they have worth that they hardly have time to think about ministry. Ministry involves being sensitive to the needs of others, reaching out, and becoming involved with loving them.

This world is full of people aching to receive a personal valentine from you. Like you, they want to know they are loved. Like you, they need to know they have worth. And you know what? You have the words they need to hear. You've found the One who loves you more than any human being ever could, who was willing to lay down His life for you that you might find forgiveness for sin and freedom to live the abundant life, today and forever.

Will you make an act of your will and repent from your self-centered attitude today? Will you begin to embrace instead a world that needs to hear the hopeful, good news of salvation? Will you take the time to hold a brother or sister's hand when they're hurting, or help carry the load of service or emotional baggage they can no longer bear alone?

Believe me, the hunger you have to feel worthwhile, loved, and complete as a human being will be satisfied when you begin to look beyond yourself and reach out to others with God's love.

STUDY **6** GUIDE

Questions for Knowing and Growing

141 1. What, according to this chapter, is the special opportunity presented to you in your singleness?

2 2. How can you begin to know what this purpose is?

3-144 3. What does Mike say to those who have a seemingly lackluster background?

147 4. Why is vision important to pursuing God's call upon your life?

147 5. What happens to people who lack vision?

148   6. What, conversely, does a vision do for the Christian?

148   7. Name the three ways in which a vision can be revealed.

150   8. Once you have that vision, how do you progress toward it?

150   9. What are goals?

150   10. Describe, in your own words, how a goal differs from a vision.

150   11. What other things, besides stepping toward our vision, do goals provide for us?

151   12. What is another way of defining a goal?

▶ 13. Reflect upon God's formative design of your life. How can you see the various factors of your upbringing—family, neighborhood, religious training, education, and so on—being knit together in the purposes of God?

Doing the Word

1. Set a challenging objective for yourself—one that requires you to depend on God's supply. That may be working with children, if you find that uncomfortable; sharing a testimony in front of your congregation; or developing a relationship with someone new at church. Allow the Lord to take leadership in the activity, and seek His strength and equipping in prayer. Then, step out, leaning completely on Him for your success.

2. Make a list of all your attributes, abilities, experiences, forms of education, and your religious, family, and community background. Are there some constant themes you can recognize which will give you clues to the call God has placed upon your life? Make a point to pray about them, then seek confirmation as discussed in this chapter.

3. Take a look at what you believe God wants you to be. Write down some goals you can achieve right now that will bring you a few steps closer to your long-range objective. Begin stepping out in His purposes for you today.

THE ARMY OF GOD

You are part of a mighty army God is raising up to
spearhead the greatest revival the world has ever seen.

WHEN I FIRST GOT INVOLVED IN SINGLES MINISTRY, I wondered why. *What was I doing here in the first place?* I knew that many people were single today because of the breakdown of the family. Divorce, immorality, and unfaithfulness were destroying more men and women than ever before. I also knew Satan was at the root of this destruction. So, I wondered, *Why would God want me involved in something that was so obviously the work of Satan? Shouldn't I be doing something to build up families instead? Shouldn't I be doing something to reclaim what was lost through Satan's deceptions and destructive measures?*

As I pondered this, the Lord reminded me of the story of Joseph. Here was a young man to whom God had given a vision of great leadership but who, along the way, seemed to suffer only hardship.

Later, when Joseph became a leader in Pharaoh's court, a famine struck the land, and many people came to him for aid. His brothers, who had treated him so harshly before, were among them.

At first, the brothers didn't know who he was. Then, Joseph revealed himself to them and they became immediately afraid. Would the brother they had so hatefully abused now turn on them in vengeance?

161

We know from the account in Genesis that he didn't. Instead, he forgave them and granted them a share in the abundance of material wealth that God had given him. But the brothers continued to fear his retaliation and, even when Joseph was near death, remained afraid.

Shortly before he died, Joseph made a final attempt to lay those fears to rest and tried to reassure them with these words:

> *You intended to harm me, but God intended it for good to accomplish what is now being done, the saving of many lives. So then, don't be afraid. I will provide for you and your children.* (Genesis 50:20–21 NIV)

The words *"You intended to harm me, but God intended it for good"* reverberated in my mind. I read it again. Then, the Lord began to speak: "Satan meant it for evil, but I meant it for good."

In a flash, I understood why God wanted me involved with single adults. Though Satan had indeed dealt destructively with families, God had it in mind to use that thing for good. He wanted to use those people—always single, widowed, and divorced—for His glory. He wanted to redeem them and use them to produce a bountiful harvest for His kingdom.

> Suddenly, in my mind, I saw before me a vast field of single adults, an army of believers capable of wholehearted, undistracted devotion to Him.

Suddenly, in my mind, I saw before me a vast field of single adults, an army of believers capable of wholehearted, undistracted devotion to Him. Empowered and sent forth by God's Spirit, they were capable of spearheading the greatest revival the world had ever known.

You, as a single adult, are a part of that mighty plan. You are a special tool in the hand of God, a finely crafted instrument who, mobilized by His Spirit, is capable of doing great things for the furtherance of His kingdom.

Unlike a teenager or a college student, you are trained and experienced in a particular field. You have talents and abilities honed over many years. You are not a person on your way to becoming a doctor, nurse, teacher, business manager, secretary, mechanic, or home manager. You are *already* established, actively practicing in an area of expertise. Just imagine what God could do with a person like you—and there are thousands of single adults like you in the world today—if you took hold of Paul's challenge and gave yourself wholly unto the Lord.

David's mighty men were people like that.

> *All these, being men of war, who could draw up in battle formation, came to Hebron with a perfect heart to make David king over all Israel; and all the rest also of Israel were of one mind to make David king.* (1 Chronicles 12:38)

Today, when we read the word "perfect," we think of something without flaw. But that's not the way the writer of Chronicles meant it. When he used the word, it meant "whole," or "complete." David's mighty men were wholehearted men. They were completely committed to David, with no reservations. And because of this unwavering devotion, there was nothing they couldn't do. Because there was nothing else vying for their affections, they were able to give themselves completely to the task set before them and conquer even their greatest enemies in the name of their God.

I believe God is grooming you even now for a place in His army. I believe He is calling you to become wholeheartedly devoted to Him—to leave all distractions behind and serve Him 100 percent.

Why? Because only the person who has left all else behind— who has said, "God, You mean more to me than the home I've lived in for years, the people I've come to know and love, and the plans

I've made for my career and my personal life"—can truly serve the Lord with all his heart. If there is anything else on the back burner of his heart, it will sap strength from his commitment to God and may cause him, ultimately, to wander away from serving God. It may even cause him to backslide.

Remember the girl I described back in chapter three? That was her problem. She desired marriage more than Jesus Christ. And even though she was bearing much fruit in ministry, she gave it all up when the opportunity to fulfill that desire came up.

God doesn't want that to happen to you. That's why He's so concerned about developing an undivided heart in you. He wants you to be completely free to serve Him—and not to be in danger of losing relationship with Him altogether.

God is calling you to be a member of His army and to serve Him with an undivided heart. And, in order to bring you to that place, He's allowing you to go through all kinds of struggles in your walk with Him.

Whether you're struggling with low self-esteem or the pain of past abuses, with raising your children alone or dealing with the death of your spouse, with getting along with others in your church or doing a good job at work, God is trying to do something in your life. He's trying to train you for service in His army—the army of God.

God wants to use your abilities, talents, skills, and experiences to change the world. He wants you to pour out everything you have before Him in service. Whether you're a secretary, a businessperson, a carpenter, an advertising executive, or a homemaker, God wants to use you. He has a place for you in His army.

In a familiar passage of 1 Corinthians, Paul said:

> *For the body is not one member, but many. If the foot should say, "Because I am not a hand, I am not a part of the body,"*

it is not for this reason any the less a part of the body. And if the ear should say, "Because I am not an eye, I am not a part of the body," it is not for this reason any the less a part of the body. If the whole body were an eye, where would the hearing be? If the whole were hearing, where would the sense of smell be? But now God has placed the members, each one of them, in the body, just as He desired. (1 Corinthians 12:14–18)

You have been given abilities, just as God desired. You have been equipped for a purpose. If your skill is typing, then you should type. If you can carry a tune, then sing. If you're mechanically inclined, then serve the Lord and the body with your skills. If you've got the gift of leadership, then use it to the glory of God.

You are part of the army of God, which is moving out to transform the world. You are part of a mighty movement that will not—and cannot—be quenched.

God is calling forth His mighty army, a battalion of highly motivated single adults devoted to serving Him. He is looking for those who are willing to give all they have, the best they have, and whatever they have for His kingdom and His purposes. He is calling you today. Will you answer the call to service? Will you give Him 100 percent? Or will you put down this book and walk away? The choice is yours.

> God is calling forth His mighty army, a battalion of highly motivated single adults devoted to serving Him.

Transitional Thought

Big and Little

Joan Kamienski was dissatisfied. She had a good job as a teacher in the local public school district, which paid a more than adequate salary. She was involved in several different programs at her local church. She even had a solid network of friends. But something was missing, and she knew it.

Seeking the Lord in prayer over a series of months, Joan began to sense that God wanted to do something bigger in her life. It wasn't that her work or involvement in church weren't important kingdom business. Joan knew they were, and she found joy in both. But somewhere, deep inside her five-foot, blonde-haired frame, she knew God wanted her in full-time ministry.

A friend directed her to a national program her denomination sponsored that connected Christians with opportunities for long- and short-term service. An opportunity to serve as an elementary school teacher in Okinawa, Japan, caught her eye, and she applied. Within a few short months, she received approval for time off from her regular job and went overseas with a commitment to serve at the school for one year.

Many things touched and amused Joan during her time in Okinawa. She was moved by the needs of the children she taught, "half halves" or part Japanese/part American kids who, because they were of mixed heritage, were the victims of deep prejudice.

The rejection even extended to schooling. They were not permitted to attend regular Japanese public schools with their fully Japanese peers. Yet God was working all things together for good, Joan noted, because many of them, as a result, chose to attend the church school, where they heard the Word of God, often for the first time.

Shopping for groceries was also a challenge. Not knowing the language, Joan was often forced to open packages in the store to sniff the contents so she knew what she was buying.

Big Fish in a Little Pond

But Joan's greatest amusement had to do with her stature. In the United States, Joan was a little person, often among the shortest in a group. But in Japan, she was big—often taller than most of the other adults she worked and lived with.

Many singles feel small in their normal environments. They view their talents and abilities as insignificant in comparison to other "big fish" in the Christian sea. Yet, given a change of circumstances, that view could instantly change. Because Joan was in Japan, all of a sudden, she wasn't small anymore. She was big. But nothing had really changed about Joan. She was still only about five feet tall, small-boned and blonde, with the same amount of gifts and abilities she had always had.

Sometimes we allow the circumstances we face to color our attitude about our abilities. Because we happen to be a little fish in a big pond, we look at our talents and skills as though they were nothing. If, on the other hand, we were in a smaller group and nobody but us could do something, suddenly we would feel we were "big," talented, and so on. But actually nothing has changed. We're still the same person with the same gifts and abilities, still able to touch God to the same degree. Only our perspective has changed.

Today I would like to challenge you to take stock of the abilities God has given you. Don't minimize them. Don't compare them with the abilities others have. Instead, begin to find ways to use them. You'll be amazed what God can do with you, as you do what you can for Him, wholeheartedly, undistractedly, as an active member of His army.

You're already enlisted. You've been given the tools to serve. Now, act on them. God will be with you.

STUDY **7** GUIDE

Questions for Knowing and Growing

[161] 1. What were Mike's original thoughts when he first considered pursuing a ministry to single adults?

[161-162] 2. Whose life story from the Old Testament did God use to help Mike understand His purpose in reaching out to singles?

3. What phrase had a specific impact on Mike?

▶ 4. What experiences, talents, or abilities do you already possess? How can God use them in His army? How can you use them in your local church, specifically?

2 | 5. What vision of single adults did Mike receive when he finally understood God's purpose?

163 | 6. What is the primary characteristic of David's mighty men that Mike says is an essential ingredient for single adults to have?

163 | 7. What does the word "perfect" mean?

165 | 8. Mike says that every single has a part to play in God's army. What Scripture verses does he use to support his point?

▶ 9. Mike believes that God is grooming you right now for a place in His army. Through what means—circumstances, individuals, and so on—can you see Him accomplishing this in your life today?

► 10. Reflect on the need to have an undivided heart. Are there parts of your life that need to be surrendered? What makes you hold on to them so tightly? What kind of things might you do that would help you "let go"?

Doing the Word

Look around you and identify needs you can meet today in your church, at your place of employment, or in relationships with family and friends. Make a list and start walking in wholehearted service to God, doing whatever your hands find to do, today.

FINAL INSTRUCTIONS

THROUGHOUT THIS BOOK, I HAVE SHARED WITH YOU the principles that will release you for wholehearted service to God. Only in centering your life upon Jesus Christ and finding your fulfillment in Him will you find release. Surrendering all that you have and the best that you have to Him will free you to give Him undistracted devotion. I have told you that it is in doing what you can do that you will find the meaning you seek. And I have told you that God's purpose for your life can be found within the person He has created you to be.

But the future lies in your hands. It is you who will choose how you respond to your singleness. It is you who will choose whether you live your life in a holding pattern, waiting for that special someone to come along, or live for the most special Someone, Jesus Christ. You will decide which you love best—some object of desire or Jesus Christ. It is you, and you alone, who will determine the outcome.

God has provided a way out of your loneliness. He has provided a way for you to be fulfilled and complete. God has designed a special purpose for you that you can begin fulfilling right now.

But He cannot force it upon you; nor does He want to. He gave you a free will to choose Him or not to choose Him—to choose His way or your own. That is as viable today as before you accepted Christ. You can choose.

Remember what Jesus said: *"He who saves his life will lose it, but whoever loses his life for My sake and the gospel's will save it"* (Mark 8:35).

Your singleness can be an experience frustrated by unfulfilled dreams, shattered hopes, vain imaginings, discouragement, doubt, and fear. Or, received as the opportunity for service that it is, it can become a fertile valley of completeness, joy, purpose, godly ambition, and fruitfulness. It is your choice. Choose today whom you will serve.

Conclusion

Now that you've read this book and completed your studies, reexamine what you believe to be God's will for you as a single person. Write down that vision, as you see it today, in the space provided below. Then, compare it to your first version at the beginning of this book. What does the comparison tell you about yourself, what you've learned, and how you've grown as a result of this study?

God's will for me as a single adult:

_____

_____

_____

_____

_____

_____

ABOUT THE AUTHOR

A motivating speaker who is known for his clarity, humor, and use of illustration, Mike Cavanaugh has traveled extensively in the U.S. and overseas. Due to his broad leadership experience and heart to equip church leaders, Mike finds himself increasingly invited to speak at pastors' and leadership events.

tograph by Neil Cowley, 2008

Mike recently completed twenty years as the pastor of Elim Gospel Church, a congregation of almost one thousand located in upstate Lima, New York. He has appeared on *The 700 Club* and the Trinity Broadcasting Network. He has also been a frequent guest lecturer at Christ for the Nations Institute in Dallas, Texas, and has spoken at several Christian festivals, including Creation, Fishnet, and Kingdom Bound.

Mike is the founder of B.A.S.I.C. (Brothers and Sisters in Christ), a local church-based college ministry, and Mobilized To Serve (M.T.S.), a nationwide single adult ministry. B.A.S.I.C. was established in 1980 to aid local churches in reaching out to college campuses in their area. The ministry currently serves students on many campuses. Mobilized To Serve (M.T.S.) was formed in 1981 to "equip and mobilize singles for service in the Body of Christ." Since then, more than fifty thousand single adults in both the U.S.

and Canada—including the divorced, the widowed, and single parents—have attended its conferences and singles days.

Mike has served as instructor of evangelism and preaching at Elim Bible Institute (EBI) and is currently on the EBI Board of Directors. He is vice president of Elim Fellowship, an association of 850 pastors, ministers, missionaries, and one hundred affiliated churches.

A graduate of EBI and Roberts Wesleyan College, Mike is continuing his studies in the Doctor of Ministry program at Bakke Graduate School in Seattle, Washington. He and his wife, Terri, reside in Lima, New York, and have three adult children.

To contact Mike Cavanaugh to speak at your church or singles group, e-mail him at mpcpastor@aol.com.